Nicola Sugden

KiDS'
little party cakes

THE AUSTRALIAN
Women's Weekly

KiDS'
little party cakes

70 clever cakes for kids of all ages

acp
books

Contents

4
games
page 102

6
wacky
page 142

5
numbers
page 122

= easy

= a little harder

= a little harder still

Critters

equipment

deep 30cm-round cake pan
2 x 9-hole (½-cup/125ml) friand pans
50cm-round prepared cake board
(see *basic know-how number 1,*
page 160)

cake

2½ x 470g packets buttercake mix
1½ quantities butter cream (page 180)
dark brown and caramel food colouring

decorations

1 tablespoon orange sprinkles
4 x 50g Violet Crumble bars
3 giant white marshmallows
2 green Smarties
5cm piece black licorice strap
1 red sour strap
3 x 30cm (3mm) black chenille sticks
(pipe cleaners), halved

1 Preheat oven to 180°C/160°C fan-forced. Grease and line round cake pan (see *basic know-how, numbers 3-6,* pages 160-161); grease friand pans.

2 Make one cake according to directions on packet. Spread mixture into round cake pan; bake about 40 minutes. Stand cake in pan 5 minutes; turn, top-side down, onto wire rack to cool.

3 Combine remaining cake mixes and make cake according to directions on packets. Drop 2½ level tablespoons of the mixture into each friand hole; bake about 20 minutes. Stand cakes in pans 5 minutes; turn, top-side up, onto wire rack to cool.

4 Transfer one-third of the butter cream to a small bowl; tint dark brown. Tint remaining two-thirds of the butter cream caramel.

5 Position large cake on prepared board; spread about three-quarters of the caramel butter cream over top and side of cake.

6 Cut a 1cm slice from the bottom of each small cake (see *step-by-step number 1,* page 166); reserve slices. Spread remaining caramel butter cream over bottoms and sides of eight of the reserved slices; top with orange sprinkles. Discard remaining slices. Using picture as a guide, position slices on large cake to make the lion's nose and cheeks (see *step-by-step number 2,* pages 166-167).

7 Spread dark brown butter cream over tops of small cakes; position around lion's face. Cut Violet Crumble bars into thin shards, use for lion's mane.

8 Using scissors, snip the tops from two marshmallows; place, cut-side up, for eyes, top with Smarties. Cut the licorice into a semi-circle for the lion's nose.

9 Cut red sour strap into a semi-circle to make the lion's mouth. Using scissors, cut two large triangles from remaining marshmallow for teeth; place at corner of mouth. Position chenille sticks for whiskers.

larry lion

This king of the jungle cake will be a hit with young explorers at a jungle-themed safari.

tips You'll have about 1 cup of cake mixture left over; use this to make extra cakes for the guests.
If the weather is wet or humid, chop the Violet Crumble bars and position them on the cake just before the party, as the damp air will make them sticky.

These cakes would work well for an Australian-themed outback party; maybe make one bush buddy for each guest.

equipment
6-hole (¾-cup/180ml) texas muffin pan
1 texas muffin paper case

cake
470g packet buttercake mix
½ quantity fluffy frosting (page 180)
½ quantity butter cream (page 180)
black and brown food colouring

decorations
koala
1 Milk Arrowroot biscuit,
    halved crossways
1 white marshmallow,
    halved crossways
2 blue mini M&M's
1 small solid milk chocolate egg
3cm piece licorice strap,
    cut into a thin strip

cockatoo
2 brown mini M&M's
1 triangular black jube,
    halved crossways
6 banana lollies

echidna
2 yellow mini M&M's
12 thin mint sticks, halved
1 chocolate malt stick, halved

wombat
2 green mini M&M's
1 clinker, halved crossways
5cm piece black licorice strap

1 Preheat oven to 180°C/160°C fan-forced. Line one hole of the texas muffin pan with the paper case; grease three pan holes.

2 Make cake according to directions on packet. Pour ⅓ cup of the mixture into the paper case and greased pan holes; bake about 25 minutes. Stand cakes in pan 5 minutes; turn, top-side up, onto wire rack to cool.

3 Transfer half the fluffy frosting to a small bowl; use black colouring to tint frosting grey. Leave remaining frosting white. Tint the butter cream brown.

bush buddies

1 koala

Shape biscuit halves into rounded shapes for ears. Spread grey frosting over top of cake in paper case and over top and edges of both ears. Using picture as a guide, position ears on cake; top ears with marshmallow halves. Position remaining decorations to make koala's eyes, nose and mouth.

2 cockatoo

Level one cake top; turn cake cut-side down. Trim cake into a rounded oval shape (see *step-by-step number 3, page 167*). Spread white frosting over the cake. Using picture as a guide, decorate cake using the lollies for the cockatoo.

3 echidna

Level one cake top; turn cake cut-side down. Trim cake into a tear-drop shape (see *step-by-step number 4*, page 166). Spread brown butter cream over the cake. Using picture as a guide, decorate cake using the lollies for the echidna.

4 wombat

Level one cake top; turn cake cut-side down. Trim cake into a rounded oval shape (see *step-by-step number 5*, pages 166-167). Spread brown butter cream over the cake. Using picture as a guide, decorate cake using the lollies for the wombat. Use a fork to mark frosting for a "furry" look.

tips The cockatoo and koala will lose their gloss after an hour or so as the frosting sets like a meringue.
You will have a small amount of cake mixture left over – barely enough for one more cake.

cheeky frogs in a pond

equipment
3-litre (12-cup) dish (see tip, below)
6-hole (⅓-cup/80ml) standard
   muffin pan

cake
470g packet buttercake mix
1 quantity butter cream (page 180)
green food colouring

decorations
4 x 85g packets blue jelly crystals
35g tube mini M&M's
10 round peppermints
10cm piece black licorice strap
5 red Smarties
5 digestive biscuits
green decorating gel
6 ready-made icing flowers

1 Make jelly according to packet directions, pour into 3-litre dish; refrigerate until set.

2 Preheat oven to 180°C/160°C fan-forced. Grease five holes of the muffin pan.

3 Make cake according to directions on packet. Drop 2½ level tablespoons of the mixture into each greased hole; bake about 20 minutes. Stand cakes in pan 5 minutes; turn, top-side up, onto wire rack to cool.

4 Level cake tops so they are the same height. Turn cakes cut-side down; trim cakes to give a rounded appearance (see *step-by-step number 35*, pages 172-173).

5 Tint the butter cream a medium green colour. Use three-quarters of the butter cream to spread over the rounded tops of the cakes.

6 Secure mini M&M's to peppermints with a little butter cream; position on frogs for eyes. Trim, shape and position thin strips of licorice strap to make mouths; position red Smarties to make tongues. Decorate frogs with more mini M&M's.

7 Trim each biscuit carefully into the shape of a lily pad (see *step-by-step number 6*, page 167). Tint remaining butter cream a darker green; spread over one side of each biscuit, scrape away any excess butter cream from around the sides of the biscuits. Top each biscuit with a frog. Use decorating gel to outline top of each lily pad.

8 Place the frogs on the set jelly; decorate the pond with the flowers.

tips We used a 35cm x 45cm oval plastic serving platter for the pond; a shallow cake pan, baking dish or shallow casserole dish would also work depending on the number of frogs you need for the party. You will have about 1 cup of cake mixture left over – enough for another five frogs.

caterpillar

Make the caterpillar as long as you like; a cake for each guest will keep everybody happy.

equipment

2 x 6-hole (¾-cup/180ml) texas
  muffin pans
25cm x 60cm prepared cake board
  (see *basic know-how number 2*,
  pages 160-161)

cake

470g packet buttercake mix
1 quantity butter cream (page 180)
red, yellow, blue and green
  food colouring

decorations

1 x 30cm (3mm) green chenille stick
  (pipe cleaner)
2 x 30cm (3mm) orange chenille sticks
  (pipe cleaners)
blue, red, yellow and green Smarties
8cm black licorice strap,
  cut into thin strips
150g packet rainbow choc-chips

1 Preheat oven to 170°C/150°C fan-forced. Grease nine holes of the texas muffin pans.

2 Make cake according to directions on packet. Drop ⅓ cup of the mixture into each greased hole; bake about 30 minutes. Stand cakes in pans 5 minutes; turn, top-side up, onto wire rack to cool.

3 Level tops of cakes so they are the same height. Cut a small crescent shape (see *step-by-step number 7*, page 166) from the sides of eight cakes.

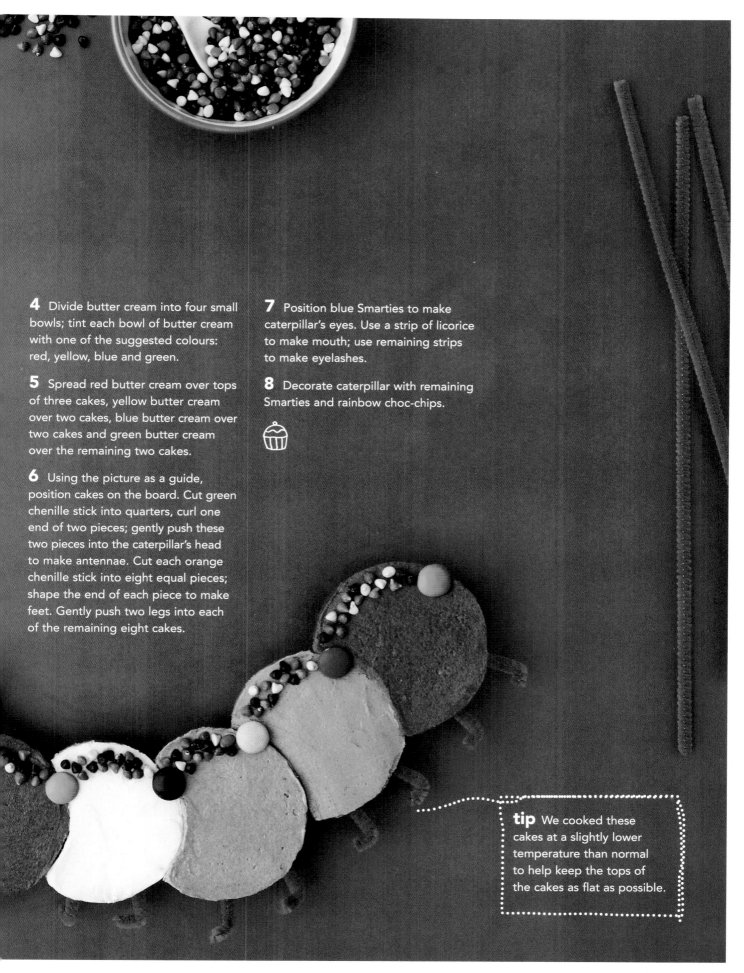

4 Divide butter cream into four small bowls; tint each bowl of butter cream with one of the suggested colours: red, yellow, blue and green.

5 Spread red butter cream over tops of three cakes, yellow butter cream over two cakes, blue butter cream over two cakes and green butter cream over the remaining two cakes.

6 Using the picture as a guide, position cakes on the board. Cut green chenille stick into quarters, curl one end of two pieces; gently push these two pieces into the caterpillar's head to make antennae. Cut each orange chenille stick into eight equal pieces; shape the end of each piece to make feet. Gently push two legs into each of the remaining eight cakes.

7 Position blue Smarties to make caterpillar's eyes. Use a strip of licorice to make mouth; use remaining strips to make eyelashes.

8 Decorate caterpillar with remaining Smarties and rainbow choc-chips.

tip We cooked these cakes at a slightly lower temperature than normal to help keep the tops of the cakes as flat as possible.

baby bluebirds

This is a cute idea for a younger child, or for an older child who has a bird as a pet. If you like, make, or buy, a larger cake and fill it with enough birds to represent the child's age.

equipment

12-hole (⅓-cup/80ml) standard
  muffin pan
deep 20cm-round cake pan
30cm-round prepared cake board (see
  basic know-how number 1, page 160)

cake

470g packet buttercake mix
1½ quantities butter cream (page 180)
¼ cup (25g) cocoa powder
blue food colouring

decorations

200g packet chocolate finger biscuits
3 x 30g Flake bars, broken into pieces
6 orange mini M&M's
4 dark chocolate Melts
1 sour worm, halved
2 mint leaves

1 Preheat oven to 180°C/160°C fan-forced. Grease 3 holes of the muffin pan. Grease and line round cake pan (see *basic know-how numbers 3-6, pages 160-161*).

2 Make cake according to directions on packet. Drop 2½ level tablespoons of the mixture into greased muffin pan holes; bake about 20 minutes. Spread remaining mixture into round cake pan; bake about 30 minutes. Stand cakes in pans 5 minutes; turn, top-side up, onto wire rack to cool.

3 Cut a 15cm circle in the top of the large cake; hollow out to make nest 2cm deep.

4 Stir two-thirds of the butter cream and the sifted cocoa powder in a small bowl until smooth. Tint remaining butter cream with the blue colouring.

5 Spread chocolate butter cream all over top, side and hollow of birds' nest. Position on prepared board; secure with a little butter cream.

6 Cut about half the biscuits in half; decorate nest with all of the biscuits and pieces of Flake.

7 Level small cake tops so they are the same height. Turn cakes cut-side down; trim cakes to give a rounded appearance (see *step-by-step number 35, page 172-173*). Spread rounded tops of cakes with blue butter cream. Position cakes in nest.

8 Using picture as a guide, position mini M&M's for birds' eyes. Cut beaks from chocolate Melts; place in position. Position sour worm in bird's beak. Decorate nest with mint leaves.

smiley starfish

equipment

6-hole (¾-cup/180ml) texas muffin pan
7 x 12-hole (1-tablespoon/20ml)
   mini muffin pans
1 yellow texas muffin paper case
77 yellow mini muffin paper cases
50cm-square prepared cake board
   (see *basic know-how number 2*,
      pages 160-161)

cake

470g packet buttercake mix
1 quantity butter cream (page 180)
yellow food colouring

decorations

85g packet yellow jelly crystals
400g packet Smarties
1 tablespoon orange sprinkles
5cm piece black licorice strap
25 white Fizzers

1 Preheat oven to 180°C/160°C fan-forced. Line texas muffin pan with the texas paper case; line mini muffin pans with the mini paper cases.

2 Make cake according to directions on packet. Drop ⅓ cup of the mixture into the texas paper case; bake about 25 minutes. Drop 2 level teaspoons of the mixture into each mini paper case; bake about 15 minutes. Stand cakes in pans 5 minutes; turn, top-side up, onto wire rack to cool.

3 Divide butter cream equally into three small bowls; tint each bowl of butter cream with yellow colouring to give three varying shades of yellow (light, medium and dark).

4 Spread light yellow butter cream over the tops of 25 cakes; sprinkle lightly with the yellow jelly crystals; top each with a yellow Smartie.

5 Spread the medium yellow butter cream over the tops of 27 cakes; sprinkle lightly with orange sprinkles.

6 Spread the dark yellow butter cream over the top of the large cake; position and secure on the prepared board with a little butter cream. Use brown Smarties for eyes, and a small piece of licorice strap for the mouth.

7 Spread remaining dark yellow butter cream over the tops of the remaining small cakes; top each with a Fizzer. Using picture as a guide, position and secure small cakes to the board with a little butter cream (see *step-by-step number 8*, pages 166-167).

tip We used 77 mini muffin sized cakes for the starfish – use more or less to get the shape you like best. Stand the cake mixture at room temperature while you bake the cakes in batches.

felicity fish

If you want to create an under-the-sea theme for a party, cover the table with a blue cloth, cut out some waves from paper and place them over the cloth. Make fishing lines using chopsticks and string, and attach sour worms for the guests to eat.

equipment

deep 20cm-round cake pan
2 x 12-hole shallow round-based
  (1½-tablespoons/30ml) patty pans
35cm-square prepared cake board
  (see *basic know-how number 2*,
  pages 160-161)

cake

470g packet buttercake mix
1½ quantities butter cream (page 180)
blue, green, purple and black
  food colouring

decorations

1 packet green hundreds
  and thousands
purple edible glitter
silver edible glitter
60g jar silver cachous
1 green mini M&M
1 round peppermint
6 pink mini M&M's

1 Preheat oven to 170°C/150°C fan-forced. Grease and line round cake pan (see *basic know-how numbers 3-6*, pages 160-161); grease 14 holes of the patty pans.

2 Make cake according to directions on packet. Spread 2 level cups of the mixture into round cake pan; bake about 30 minutes. Drop 3 level teaspoons of mixture into the greased patty pan holes; bake about 10 minutes. Stand cakes in pans 5 minutes; turn, top-side up, onto wire rack to cool.

3 Using paper pattern, from pattern sheet provided, cut a 1cm-deep curve on the large cake for the fish's face (see *step-by-step numbers 9-10*, pages 167-168). Cut the 1cm slice of cake in one piece away from the fish's body (see *step-by-step number 10*, page 168); reserve slice.

4 Using paper pattern, from pattern sheet provided, cut out a tail and two fins from reserved cake slice (see *step-by-step number 11*, pages 168-169).

5 Tint two-thirds of the butter cream blue; spread all over top and sides of cake, fins and tail. Using picture as a guide, position cakes on board.

6 Divide remaining butter cream into three small bowls; tint one bowl green, another bowl purple, and use a little black colouring to tint the remaining bowl grey.

7 Spread green butter cream over tops of five small cakes. Spread purple butter cream over tops of five small cakes, and spread the grey butter cream over tops of four small cakes.

8 Roll the tops of the green cakes in the hundreds and thousands. Lightly sprinkle the five purple cakes with the purple glitter. Lightly sprinkle the grey cakes with the silver glitter.

9 Using picture as a guide, position the small cakes on fish's body, slightly overlapping each row with the next.

10 Sprinkle tail lightly with purple glitter; decorate the tail and fins with silver cachous. Secure green mini M&M to peppermint with a little butter cream; position on fish for eye. Position the pink mini M&M's for the fish's mouth.

equipment

6-hole (¾-cup/180ml) texas
  muffin pan
prepared cake board
  (see introduction)

cake

470g packet buttercake mix
½ quantity butter cream (page 180)
red food colouring

decorations

1 black licorice strap
1 x 35g tube mini M&M's

1 Preheat oven to 180°C/160°C fan-forced. Grease texas muffin pan.

2 Make cake according to directions on packet. Drop ⅓ cup of the mixture into each hole; bake about 25 minutes. Stand cakes in pan 5 minutes; turn, top-side up, onto wire rack to cool.

3 Level tops of cakes so they are the same height. Turn cakes cut-side down onto a board. Trim cakes to give a rounded appearance (see *step-by-step number 35*, pages 172-173).

4 Tint butter cream red; spread cakes all over with butter cream.

If you make a ladybird for each guest, place them on individual prepared cake boards or plates (about 8cm diameter). Or, you might prefer the ladybirds together, with some leaves, on a large prepared cake board, platter or cake stand.

ladybirds

5 Using picture as a guide, cut six semi-circles from licorice strap, position for faces. Cut remaining licorice strap into thin strips; position one strip down the centre of each ladybird's body.

6 Use a little butter cream to attach two red mini M&M's to each face to make eyes. Use remaining mini M&M's to decorate ladybirds.

tips Push a small fork (or cake fork) into the bottom of each cake to make handling and icing the cakes easier. You will have enough cake mixture left over to make three more cakes.

pigs in mud

Youngsters will squeal with delight at the sight of these cute little pigs. You could easily make a piglet for each small guest to take home.

equipment
12-hole (⅓-cup/80ml) standard muffin pan
deep 30cm-round cake pan
40cm-round prepared cake board (see *basic know-how number 1*, page 160)

cake
2 x 470g packets buttercake mix
2 quantities butter cream (page 180)
pink food colouring
½ cup (50g) cocoa powder

decorations
2 x 200g packets chocolate finger biscuits
4 large domed pink marshmallows
8 brown mini M&M's
12 pink Mallow Bakes
1 x 30cm (3mm) pink chenille stick (pipe cleaner), quartered
2 square-based ice-cream cones
1 tablespoon yellow sugar crystals (see tip, page 25)
1 tablespoon blue sugar crystals (see tip, page 25)

1 Preheat oven to 180°C/160°C fan-forced. Grease four holes of the muffin pan. Grease and line the round cake pan (see *basic know-how numbers 3-6*, pages 160-161).

2 Make cake according to directions on packets. Drop 2½ level tablespoons of the mixture into greased muffin pan holes; bake about 20 minutes. Pour remaining mixture into round pan; bake about 40 minutes. Stand cakes in pans 5 minutes; turn, top-side up, onto wire rack to cool.

3 Transfer a quarter of the butter cream to a small bowl; tint with pink colouring. Stir sifted cocoa powder into the remaining butter cream.

4 Level top of round cake; place cake, cut-side down, on board. Spread cake all over with chocolate butter cream. Press biscuits around side of cake.

5 Level tops of small cakes. Turn cakes cut-side down onto board. Trim cakes to give rounded shapes (see *step-by-step number 35*, pages 172-173), for pigs' bodies. Spread pink butter cream over bodies.

6 Cut and discard the small tip from each of the large marshmallows; secure marshmallows to bodies to make pigs' heads. Secure brown mini M&M's to heads for eyes with a little butter cream.

7 Halve four Mallow Bakes. Pinch halves to make ears; position on heads with a little butter cream. Position one Mallow Bake below eyes for snout; secure with a little butter cream.

8 Curl each piece of the chenille stick; position for pigs' tails.

9 Using picture as a guide, position pigs in mud. Position remaining Mallow Bakes on one pig for legs. Trim tops from ice-cream cones, if required, then fill with sugar crystals; position on cake for troughs.

tip Instead of tinting your own sugar, you can use the packets of coloured sugar crystals found in packets of Monster 5s or Fairy 5s, available from supermarkets.

octavius

equipment

20cm x 30cm lamington pan
5 x 12-hole (1-tablespoon/20ml)
   mini muffin pans
60 mini muffin paper cases (26 green,
   20 yellow, 14 orange)
50cm-square prepared cake board
   (see *basic know-how number 2*,
   pages 160-161)

cake

2 x 470g packets buttercake mix
1½ quantities butter cream (page 180)
green, orange and yellow
   food colouring

decorations

2 x 300g packets fruit rings
200g packet small jelly beans
2 blue mini M&M's
2 round peppermints
2 sour worms

1 Preheat oven to 180°C/160°C fan-forced. Grease lamington pan; line base and long sides with baking paper, extending paper 5cm over sides.

2 Make one cake according to directions on packet. Spread mixture into pan; bake about 35 minutes. Stand cake in pan 5 minutes; turn, top-side up, onto wire rack to cool.

3 Meanwhile, line mini muffin pans with the paper cases. Make remaining cake according to directions on packet. Drop 2 level teaspoons of the mixture into each paper case; bake about 15 minutes. Stand cakes in pans 5 minutes; turn, top-side up, onto wire rack to cool.

4 Level top of large cake; turn cake cut-side down. Using paper pattern, from pattern sheet provided, cut out head for octopus from cake. Position head on prepared board, cut-side down; secure with a little butter cream. Discard remaining cake.

5 Tint two-thirds of the butter cream green. Divide remaining butter cream equally into two small bowls; tint one bowl orange and the other yellow.

6 Spread two-thirds of the green butter cream all over top and sides of head; spread remaining green butter cream over the tops of 26 cakes in green cases. Spread yellow butter cream over the tops of 20 cakes in yellow cases. Spread orange butter cream over the tops of remaining cakes. Using picture as a guide, position cakes on prepared board to make tentacles; secure to board with a little butter cream.

7 Position colour-matched fruit rings on tops of small cakes.

8 Use jelly beans to outline the head. Position 2 red fruit rings for eyes; using a little butter cream secure mini M&M's onto peppermints, place on top of fruit rings. Position sour worms for mouth.

We used 42 green jelly beans to outline the head of the octopus. Stand cake mixture at room temperature while you bake the cakes in batches. You will have 1 cup of cake mixture left over – enough for another 24 mini cakes. You could add these to the cake to make longer tentacles.

pierre peacock

equipment

20cm x 30cm lamington pan
2 x 9-hole (½-cup/125ml) friand pans
12-hole (1-tablespoon/20ml)
   mini muffin pan
60cm-square prepared cake board
   (see *basic know-how number* 2,
      pages 160-161)

cake

3 x 470g packets buttercake mix
2 quantities butter cream (page 180)
blue, purple and green food colouring

decorations

51cm x 64cm piece
   dark blue cardboard
green edible glitter
7 white marshmallows
26 blue Smarties
14 purple Smarties
6 yellow mini M&M's
1 blue mini M&M
1 round peppermint
140g packet Monster 5s
2 x 30cm (3mm) gold foil chenille
   sticks (pipe cleaners)

1 Preheat oven to 180°C/160°C fan-forced. Grease lamington pan; line base and long sides with baking paper, extending paper 5cm over sides.

2 Make one cake according to directions on packet. Spread mixture into lamington pan; bake about 35 minutes. Stand cake in pan 5 minutes; turn, top-side up, onto wire rack to cool.

3 Reduce oven temperature to 170°C/150°C fan-forced. Grease 14 holes of the friand pans; grease mini muffin pan.

4 Make remaining cake according to directions on packets. Drop 2½ level tablespoons of the mixture into the greased holes of the friand pans. Bake about 20 minutes. Stand cakes in pans 5 minutes; turn, top-side up, onto wire rack to cool. Wash, dry and grease 14 holes of the friand pans. Drop 2 level tablespoons of the mixture into the greased holes of the friand pans; bake about 15 minutes. Stand cakes in pans 5 minutes; turn, top-side up, onto wire rack to cool.

5 Drop 3 level teaspoons of the mixture into the greased holes of the mini muffin pan; bake about 15 minutes. Stand cakes in pan 5 minutes; turn, top-side up, onto wire rack to cool.

6 Level top of lamington cake; turn cake cut-side down. Using paper pattern, from pattern sheet provided, cut peacock's body from cake (see *basic know-how numbers 8-9*, pages 160-161); discard remaining cake. Using pattern sheet, cut out peacock's feathers from the cardboard; place on prepared board.

7 Tint one-third of the butter cream blue using blue and purple colouring. Spread over top and sides of peacock's body. Using picture as a guide, position body on cardboard.

8 Divide remaining butter cream equally into three small bowls; tint each bowl with green colouring to give three varying shades of green (light, medium and dark). Spread dark green butter cream over tops of mini muffins; spread medium green butter cream over tops of smaller friands and spread light green butter cream over tops of larger friands. Dust with edible glitter.

9 Using picture as a guide, assemble cakes on board; position mini muffins to make first tier of feathers; position 14 small friands to make second tier of feathers. Position large friands to make final tier of feathers.

10 Cut marshmallows in half; position, cut-side down, on large friands; top each with a blue Smartie, secure with a little butter cream. Position a purple Smartie on each smaller friand, and position blue Smarties on mini muffins.

11 Position yellow mini M&M's to make peacock's beak. Secure blue mini M&M to peppermint with a little butter cream; position on peacock for eye. Sprinkle the packet of blue sugar crystals from Monster 5s over centre of peacock's body.

12 Halve one chenille stick to make peacock's legs. Cut remaining chenille stick into short pieces; position on top of head for peacock's crest.

tip You'll have 1 cup of the cake mixture left over for more little cakes for the party.

tip You'll have ½ cup of the cake mixture left over, enough for another mini loaf.

equipment

9-hole (½-cup/125ml) friand pan
8-hole (½-cup/125ml) mini loaf pan
25cm-square prepared cake board
  (see *basic know-how number 2*,
    pages 160-161)

cake

½ x 470g packet buttercake mix
½ quantity butter cream (page 180)
pink food colouring

decorations

1 pink Mallow Bake
1 strip black licorice bootlace
2 brown M&M's
3 red mini M&M's
14 white Mallow Bakes
1 diamond-shaped red jube
1 giant white marshmallow

1 Preheat oven to 170°C/150°C fan-forced. Grease three holes of the friand pan; grease one hole of the mini loaf pan.

2 Make cake according to directions on packet. Drop 2½ level tablespoons of the mixture into the greased holes of the friand pan. Drop ⅓ cup of the mixture into the greased hole of the mini loaf pan. Bake cakes about 20 minutes. Stand cakes in pans 5 minutes; turn, top-side up, onto wire rack to cool.

3 Level cake tops so they are the same height. Trim corners from the loaf cake to make an oval shape for the bunny's body.

4 Tint butter cream pink; spread over tops and sides of cakes. Using picture as a guide, position cakes on board; secure with a little butter cream.

5 Cut the pink Mallow Bake in half, trim into triangular shape for nose; position on cake. Cut 4 x 2cm pieces bootlace for whiskers and 2 x 3cm pieces for mouth; position on cake. Position brown M&M's for eyes and red M&M's for buttons. Position white Mallow Bakes on bunny's ears.

6 Split jube in half lengthways; trim to make bow tie. Use giant marshmallow for bunny's tail; secure to board with a little butter cream.

Pinky bunny is a small cute cake – just enough for a small cute person's birthday.

pinky bunny

buzzy bee

If it's too humid to make the toffee wings, shape some craft wire into the wing shapes then cover them with a yellow-tinted cellophane paper.

equipment
5 x 12-hole (1-tablespoon/20ml) mini muffin pans
12-hole (⅓-cup/80ml) standard muffin pan
2.25-litre (9-cup) pudding steamer
60 mini muffin paper cases (28 yellow, 32 dark brown)
35cm-square prepared cake board (see *basic know-how number 2*, pages 160-161)

cake
2 x 470g packets buttercake mix
1½ quantities butter cream (page 180)
yellow and black food colouring

toffee
1 cup (220g) caster sugar
½ cup (125ml) water

decorations
2 blue Smarties
5 red mini M&M's
1 x 30cm (3mm) black chenille stick (pipe cleaner)

1 Preheat oven to 180°C/160°C fan-forced. Line mini muffin pans with the paper cases. Grease one hole of the standard muffin pan.

2 Make one cake according to directions on packet. Drop 2 level teaspoons of the mixture into each mini paper case; bake about 15 minutes. Drop 2½ level tablespoons of the mixture into the greased hole of the standard muffin pan; bake about 20 minutes. Turn cakes, top-side up, onto wire rack to cool.

3 Reduce oven temperature to 170°C/150°C fan-forced. Grease pudding steamer. Make remaining cake according to directions on packet. Pour mixture into steamer; bake about 45 minutes. Stand cake in steamer 5 minutes; turn, top-side down, onto wire rack to cool.

4 Using paper pattern, from pattern sheet provided, trace two wings onto baking paper. Turn paper upside down onto an oven tray.

5 Combine sugar and the water in a small saucepan; stir over heat, without boiling, until sugar dissolves. Bring to the boil; boil, uncovered, without stirring, about 10 minutes or until toffee is golden brown. Remove from heat; allow bubbles to subside. Carefully pour toffee onto outline of wing shapes on paper (see *step-by-step number 12*, page 169); stand at room temperature until set.

6 Level top of pudding cake; place cake, cut-side down, on prepared board. Trim top of the pudding cake to make a more rounded shape.

7 Trim standard muffin cake into a more rounded shape (see *step-by-step number 35*, pages 172-173); trim one side a little flatter and secure this side to the pudding cake with a little butter cream.

8 Tint two-thirds of the butter cream yellow; tint remaining butter cream black. Spread yellow butter cream over body and head of the bee. Spread remaining yellow butter cream over tops of small cakes in the yellow paper cases. Spread black butter cream over tops of small cakes in the brown paper cases.

9 Using picture as a guide, alternate bands of yellow and black cakes to cover the bee's body.

10 Position blue Smarties for eyes and mini M&M's for mouth. Cut chenille stick in half, curl one end of each; insert into cake for antennae. Carefully insert wings into the bee's body.

tips Make the mini muffins in batches; the cake mixture will be fine to stand at room temperature.
Make the toffee wings up to 3 hours before the party. Position the wings just before the party.

fantasy

flower bouquet

We used an orange and yellow theme for the flowers, which is why we needed four jars of lollies. The bouquet is quite top-heavy, so handle gently. The chopstick is the "handle" for the bouquet.

equipment
3 x 12-hole (1-tablespoon/20ml)
  mini muffin pans
30 mini muffin paper cases
  (15 yellow, 15 orange)
1 wooden chopstick
1 x 10cm styrofoam ball
30 strong double-pointed
  wooden toothpicks

cake
½ x 470g packet buttercake mix
½ quantity butter cream (page 180)

decorations
4 x 40g jars BoPeep lollies
35g tube mini M&M's
wrapping paper
ribbon

1 Preheat oven to 180°C/160°C fan-forced. Line mini muffin pans with the paper cases.

2 Make cake according to directions on packet. Drop 2 level teaspoons of the mixture into each paper case; bake about 15 minutes. Stand cakes in pans 5 minutes; turn, top-side up, onto wire rack to cool.

3 Spread tops of cakes with butter cream. Using picture as a guide, position five BoPeep lollies and one mini M&M on each cake to make orange and yellow flowers.

4 Push the chopstick about halfway through the styrofoam ball. Place the ball into a container (such as a jug) so that two-thirds of the ball is exposed (this is where the flower cakes will go). Insert a toothpick into the ball, then gently push a cake onto the toothpick (see *step-by-step number 13*, page 168). Position cakes closely around the ball to make the bouquet. Wrap paper around the chopstick and secure with the ribbon.

tips Styrofoam balls are available from craft stores and florist shops. Use any left over cake mixture to make more little cakes for the party.

beautiful b⊙w

equipment
4 x 12-hole (1-tablespoon/20ml)
  mini muffin pans
48 mini muffin paper cases (purple)
40cm x 55cm prepared cake board
  (see *basic know-how number 2*,
  pages 160-161)

cake
½ x 470g packet buttercake mix
½ quantity butter cream (page 180)
purple food colouring

decorations
purple edible glitter
60g jar silver cachous

1 Preheat oven to 180°C/160°C
fan-forced. Line mini muffin pans
with the paper cases.

2 Make cake according to directions
on packet. Drop 2 level teaspoons of
the mixture into each paper case;
bake about 15 minutes. Stand cakes
in pans 5 minutes; turn, top-side up,
onto wire rack to cool.

3 Tint butter cream purple; spread
over tops of cakes. Sprinkle cakes
with edible glitter; decorate with
cachous. Using picture as a guide,
position cakes on prepared board in
the shape of a large bow; secure with
a little butter cream.

tip You'll have about ⅓ cup
of the cake mixture left over,
enough for another eight or
so little cakes.

tips Make one packet of cake mix at a time. Bake two trays of cakes together and, while they're baking, put the cake mixture into the next two trays – this way you'll have an efficient production line. The cakes can be made a day ahead and kept in an airtight container, or frozen, for up to three months.

rainbow

This cake is for a large party (only half the rainbow is shown here). For the best effect, match the paper cases to the colours of the rainbow, that is, to the colours of the frosting and jelly crystals. The sky background makes it fun, as does the pot of gold at the end of the rainbow.

equipment
4 x 12-hole (1-tablespoon/20ml) mini muffin pans
144 mini muffin paper cases (35 red, 33 orange, 29 green, 26 blue, 21 purple)
65cm x 1m prepared cake board (see *basic know-how number 2*, pages 160-161)

cake
4 x 470g packets buttercake mix
2 quantities fluffy mock cream frosting (page 180)
red, orange, green, blue and purple food colouring

decorations
5 x 85g packets jelly crystals (red, orange, green, blue and purple)
small gold-coloured plastic hat or pot
gold-coloured tissue paper
gold-covered chocolate coins and chocolates
cotton wool

1 Preheat oven to 180°C/160°C fan-forced. Line mini muffin pans with the paper cases.

2 Make cake according to directions on packets. Drop 2 level teaspoons of the mixture into each paper case; bake about 15 minutes. Stand cakes in pans 5 minutes; turn, top-side up, onto wire rack to cool.

3 Meanwhile, make fluffy mock cream frosting. Divide frosting equally into five small bowls; tint each bowl with one of the suggested colours: red, orange, green, blue and purple.

4 Pour the jelly crystals into separate small bowls. Match the colours of the frosting with the jelly crystals. If the crystals are too pale, make them darker by rubbing some colouring through the crystals (see *basic know-how number 25*, page 164).

5 Spread red frosting over the tops of 35 cakes; dip into red jelly crystals. Spread orange frosting over the tops of 33 cakes; dip into orange jelly crystals. Spread green frosting over the tops of 29 cakes; dip into green jelly crystals. Spread blue frosting over the tops of 26 cakes; dip into blue jelly crystals. Spread purple frosting over the tops of 21 cakes; dip into purple jelly crystals.

6 Using picture as a guide, position cakes, starting with the red ones, on prepared board. Secure the cakes to the board with a little frosting.

7 Position the pot of gold; line with tissue paper then fill with chocolate coins and chocolates. Pull pieces of cotton wool into cloud shapes and position on board.

heart cake

equipment

6 x 12-hole (1-tablespoon/20ml)
    mini muffin pans
12-hole (1/3-cup/80ml) standard
    muffin pan
64 mini muffin paper cases (brown)
1 standard paper case (brown)
6cm-round fluted cutter
3cm-round fluted cutter
45cm-square prepared cake board
    (see *basic know-how number 2*,
        pages 160-161)

cake

470g packet buttercake mix
2 tablespoons apricot jam,
    warmed, sieved
½ cup (80g) icing sugar
500g ready-made white icing
    (page 180)
pink food colouring

decorations

1 large red icing double heart
11g jar pink candy heart sprinkles

1 Preheat oven to 180°C/160°C fan-forced. Line mini muffin pans with the mini paper cases; line one hole of the standard muffin pan with the standard paper case.

2 Make cake according to directions on packet. Drop 2 level teaspoons of the mixture into each mini paper case; bake about 15 minutes. Drop 2½ level tablespoons of the mixture into the standard paper case; bake about 20 minutes. Stand cakes in pans 5 minutes; turn, top-side up, onto wire racks to cool.

3 Cutting through the paper case, trim 1.5cm from the base of the large cake.

4 Brush jam over tops of all cakes. On a surface dusted with sifted icing sugar, knead the ready-made icing until smooth; tint pink (see *basic know-how number 16*, page 162). Roll icing out to 3mm thickness. Cut one 6cm round from the icing; position on the large cake. Gently push the large red heart into the icing on the large cake.

5 Cut 64 x 3cm rounds from the icing; position on the small cakes. Brush a tiny amount of water over the tops of the small cakes; top cakes with candy heart sprinkles.

6 Using picture as a guide, position cakes on board in the shape of a heart; secure with a little butter cream.

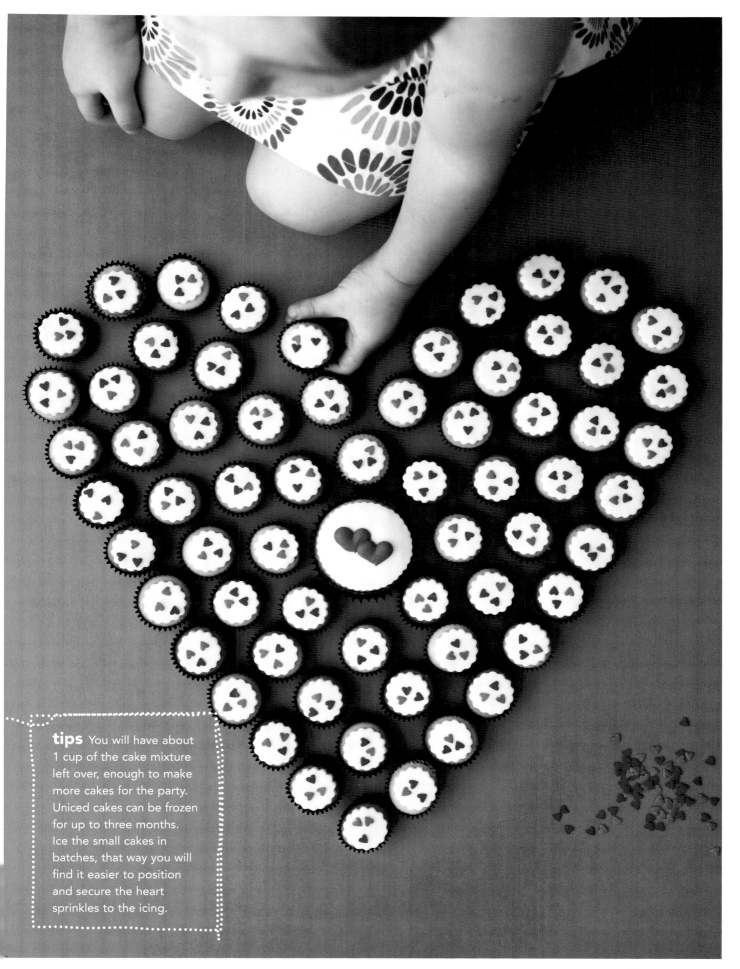

tips You will have about 1 cup of the cake mixture left over, enough to make more cakes for the party. Uniced cakes can be frozen for up to three months. Ice the small cakes in batches, that way you will find it easier to position and secure the heart sprinkles to the icing.

equipment

6-hole (¾-cup/180ml) texas muffin pan
12-hole (⅓-cup/80ml) standard
    muffin pan
12-hole (1-tablespoon/20ml)
    mini muffin pan
35cm x 55cm prepared cake board
    (see *basic know-how number 2*,
    pages 160-161)

cake

470g packet buttercake mix
1 quantity butter cream (page 180)
red, orange, yellow, green, blue and
    purple food colouring

decorations

1 triangular purple jube, halved
1 x 30cm (3mm) black chenille stick
    (pipe cleaner)
35g tube mini M&M's
410g packet Smarties

1 Preheat oven to 180°C/160°C fan-forced. Grease one hole of the texas muffin pan; grease 11 holes of the standard muffin pan; grease two holes of the mini muffin pan.

2 Make cake according to directions on packet. Drop ⅓ cup of mixture into the greased hole of the texas muffin pan. Drop 2½ level tablespoons of the mixture into the greased holes of the standard muffin pan. Drop 3 level teaspoons of mixture into the greased holes of the mini muffin pan. Bake larger cakes about 20 minutes; bake small cakes about 15 minutes. Stand cakes in pans 5 minutes; turn, top-side up, onto wire rack to cool.

3 Divide butter cream into six small bowls; tint each bowl with one of the suggested colours: red, orange, yellow, green, blue and purple.

4 Using picture as a guide, trim the side of the largest cake to make the serpent's head; spread red butter cream all over head. Trim tops of remaining cakes to make them level. Spread tops with orange, yellow, blue green, purple and red butter cream.

5 Position jube halves for eyes. Cut chenille stick into two 5cm pieces, twist together to make serpent's forked tongue; gently push into front of head. Position the cakes on prepared board; secure with a little butter cream.

6 Using picture as a guide, decorate the serpent with M&M's and Smarties.

Make the rainbow serpent as long as you like; he could be slithering along the whole length of the party table.

rainbow serpent

tip You'll have about ½ cup of the cake mixture left over; make more cakes for a longer serpent, if you like.

fairy dolls

Small dolls of a suitable size for these cakes come and go in the shops as fashions change. You might have to trim the skirts on the dolls to make it easier to insert them into the cakes.

equipment
6-hole (¾-cup/180ml) texas muffin pan
5 texas muffin paper cases
   (coloured to match the dolls)
8cm-round fluted cutter

cake
470g packet buttercake mix
2 tablespoons apricot jam,
   warmed, sieved
½ cup (80g) icing sugar
200g ready-made white icing
   (page 180)
pink, orange, yellow, green and
   blue food colouring

decorations
5 small dolls
55g jar small icing hearts

1 Preheat oven to 180°C/160°C fan-forced. Line texas muffin pan with the paper cases.

2 Make cake according to directions on packet. Drop ⅓ cup of the mixture into each paper case; bake about 25 minutes. Stand cakes in pan 5 minutes; turn, top-side up, onto wire rack to cool.

3 Brush tops of cakes with jam. On a surface dusted with sifted icing sugar, knead the ready-made icing until smooth. Divide icing into five equal portions; tint each portion with one of the suggested colours: pink, orange, yellow, green and blue (see *basic know-how number 16*, page 162). Roll each portion into a 3mm thickness; using 8cm cutter, cut one round from each portion.

4 Position icing rounds on top of cakes. Using a small pointed knife, cut a 2.5cm hole in the centre of the icing on each cake. Carefully remove and discard the icing centre. Gently push the dolls into the centre of each cake.

5 Brush a tiny amount of water on the back of the small icing hearts; position around cakes.

Buy a doll that will appeal to the birthday girl, then match the colour of the cakes and decorations to the doll's clothing.

tips We bought the ready-made flowers and the glitter from a cake decorating shop. We found the doll and cake easier to manage if we removed the legs. Her legs can easily be repositioned after the party.

equipment
1 x 2.5 litre (10-cup) dolly varden pan
6 x 12-hole (1-tablespoon/20ml) mini muffin pans
72 mini muffin paper cases (purple)
30cm-round prepared cake board
(see *basic know-how number 1*, page 160)

cake
2½ x 470g packets buttercake mix
1 quantity butter cream (page 180)
purple food colouring

decorations
28cm doll
purple edible glitter
52 purple ready-made icing flowers
67 pink ready-made icing flowers

1 Preheat oven to 180°C/160°C fan-forced. Grease the dolly varden pan well. Line mini muffin pans with the paper cases.

2 Make cake according to directions on packets. Drop 5 cups of the mixture into the dolly varden pan; bake about 1 hour. Drop 2 level teaspoons of the mixture into each paper case; bake about 15 minutes. Stand cakes in pans about 5 minutes; turn, top-side up, onto wire rack to cool.

3 Level top of large cake. Position cake on prepared board cut-side down; secure with a little butter cream. Using a teaspoon, scoop a hole from the top of the cake deep enough to fit doll; position doll in cake.

4 Tint butter cream purple. Spread half the butter cream all over large cake. Spread remaining butter cream over tops of small cakes; sprinkle each with a little glitter.

5 Using picture as a guide, position a band of small cakes at the base of the large cake, pressing each one firmly into the butter cream as you go (see *step-by-step number 14*, pages 168-169). Repeat with the remaining small cakes until there are four rows of cakes. Position the flowers on the cakes.

princess belinda

tips You'll have about 1 cup of the cake mixture left over, enough for another three handbags. Use a palette knife to position the bags on the prepared board.

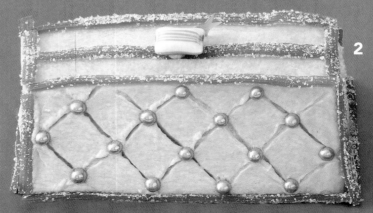
1

glambags

equipment

8-hole (½-cup/125ml) mini loaf pan
12 strong wooden toothpicks, tips broken off into 1.5cm lengths
30cm x 40cm prepared cake board (see *basic know-how number 2*, pages 160-161)

cake

470g packet buttercake mix
1 quantity butter cream (page 180)
red, pink, purple, orange, blue and white food colouring

decorations
purple bag

2 red sour straps
1 white and purple BoPeep lolly
10 small ready-made icing hearts

blue bag

1 packet blue sugar-coated bootlace
60g jar mixed cachous
1 blue and white BoPeep lolly

white bag

2 x 12cm pieces black licorice strap
1 black BoPeep lolly

red bag

14cm piece black licorice strap, cut in half lengthways
60g jar silver cachous

orange bag

1 red sour strap, cut into thin strips
1 red BoPeep lolly
5 orange BoPeep lollies

pink bag

1 red sour strap, cut into thin strips
1 pink and white BoPeep lolly
60g jar mixed cachous
1 pink ready-made icing flower

1 Preheat oven to 170°C/150°C fan-forced. Grease six holes of the mini loaf pan.

2 Make cake according to directions on packet. Drop ⅓ cup of the mixture into greased pan holes; bake about 25 minutes. Stand cakes in pan 5 minutes; turn, top-side up, onto wire rack to cool.

3 Divide butter cream equally into six small bowls; tint each with one of the suggested colours: red, pink, purple, orange, blue and white.

4 Level cake tops; turn cut-side down. Cut sides of cakes on an angle, leaving a 2cm width at the top of the cakes (see *step-by-step number 15*, page 169).

5 Spread tops and sides of each cake with one of the coloured butter creams.

2

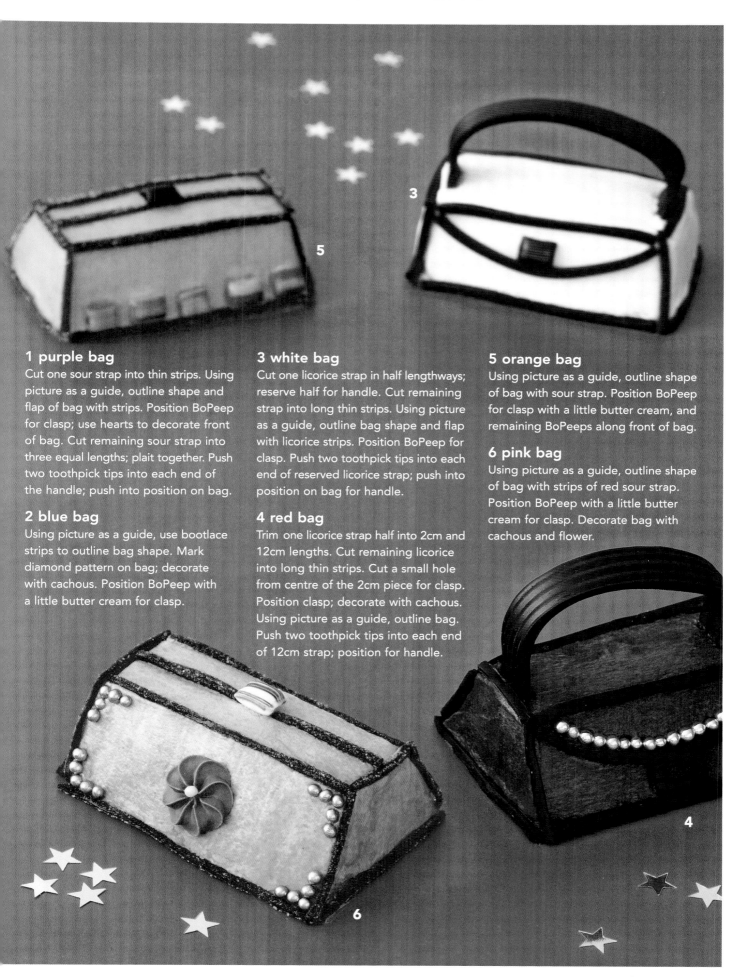

1 purple bag

Cut one sour strap into thin strips. Using picture as a guide, outline shape and flap of bag with strips. Position BoPeep for clasp; use hearts to decorate front of bag. Cut remaining sour strap into three equal lengths; plait together. Push two toothpick tips into each end of the handle; push into position on bag.

2 blue bag

Using picture as a guide, use bootlace strips to outline bag shape. Mark diamond pattern on bag; decorate with cachous. Position BoPeep with a little butter cream for clasp.

3 white bag

Cut one licorice strap in half lengthways; reserve half for handle. Cut remaining strap into long thin strips. Using picture as a guide, outline bag shape and flap with licorice strips. Position BoPeep for clasp. Push two toothpick tips into each end of reserved licorice strap; push into position on bag for handle.

4 red bag

Trim one licorice strap half into 2cm and 12cm lengths. Cut remaining licorice into long thin strips. Cut a small hole from centre of the 2cm piece for clasp. Position clasp; decorate with cachous. Using picture as a guide, outline bag. Push two toothpick tips into each end of 12cm strap; position for handle.

5 orange bag

Using picture as a guide, outline shape of bag with sour strap. Position BoPeep for clasp with a little butter cream, and remaining BoPeeps along front of bag.

6 pink bag

Using picture as a guide, outline shape of bag with strips of red sour strap. Position BoPeep with a little butter cream for clasp. Decorate bag with cachous and flower.

magic wands

A circle of magic wands on a round board is a great centrepiece for a party table. Don't be too fussy spreading the butter cream around the sides of the stars, the strips of sour straps will hide any mistakes.

equipment
20cm x 30cm lamington pan
12cm star cutter
3.5cm star cutter
36cm x 48cm prepared cake board
    (see *basic know-how number 2*,
     pages 160-161)

cake
470g packet buttercake mix
1 quantity butter cream (page 180)
pink, yellow and orange food colouring

decorations
6 fruit sticks (2 pink, 2 yellow, 2 orange)
16 red sour straps
silver edible glitter
60g jar silver cachous

1 Preheat oven to 180°C/160°C fan-forced. Grease lamington pan; line base and long sides with baking paper, extending paper 5cm over sides.

2 Make cake according to directions on packet. Spread mixture into pan; bake about 35 minutes. Stand cake in pan 5 minutes; turn onto wire rack to cool.

3 Cut six 12cm stars from the cake (see *step-by-step number 16*, page 168).

4 Divide butter cream into three small bowls; tint each with one of the suggested colours: pink, yellow and orange.

5 Spread tops and sides of two of the stars with pink butter cream; repeat with remaining stars and butter cream. Position wands on the prepared board, leaving space for the handles; secure with a little butter cream.

6 Position fruit sticks to make handles for the wands. Cut 60 x 1.5cm lengths of sour strap; position 10 pieces around sides of each star to define the shape. Place the small cutter in the centre of a star, sprinkle glitter inside the cutter; carefully remove the cutter. Repeat with remaining stars. Using picture as a guide, decorate the wands with cachous.

tips Freeze the star-shaped cakes for about an hour, this will minimise the cake crumbs mixing with the butter cream.

heart balloons

equipment
12-hole (½-cup/125ml) friand pan
5 strong wooden toothpicks
35cm x 40cm prepared cake board
(see *basic know-how number 2*,
pages 160-161)
medium gum-leaf cutter

cake
470g packet buttercake mix
1 quantity butter cream (page 180)
pink food colouring

decorations
1 x 140g packet Fairy 5s (sprinkles)
ribbons

1 Preheat oven to 170°C/150°C fan-forced. Grease 10 holes of the friand pan.

2 Make cake according to directions on packet. Drop 2½ level tablespoons of the mixture into greased pan holes; bake about 20 minutes. Stand cakes in pan 5 minutes; turn, top-side up, onto wire rack to cool.

3 Trim a small segment from each friand (see *step-by-step number 17*, pages 168-169). Secure two trimmed friands together with a toothpick. Repeat with remaining friands and toothpicks.

4 Divide butter cream evenly into three small bowls. Tint each a different shade of pink. Spread one cake with butter cream, then gently press sprinkles onto the side of the cake. Using picture as a guide, position hearts on board; secure with a little butter cream. Position gum-leaf cutter on top of the cake; sprinkle some of the sprinkles inside the cutter. Carefully remove the cutter. Repeat with the remaining cakes, butter creams and sprinkles.

5 Gently push one end of a ribbon under each cake.

tips You'll have about 1 cup of the cake mixture left over, enough to make another four balloons. The balloons are not difficult to make, but getting the sides of the cakes evenly covered with sprinkles takes a little time. An alternative would be to ice the cakes, then pick the cake up between your thumb and forefinger, roll the side of each cake into the sprinkles – then position and secure on the board. Use a spatula to smooth out your finger prints. We found it necessary to support the two pieces of cake with a toothpick. Make sure older guests remove the toothpicks before eating the cakes; remove the toothpicks before giving cakes to younger guests to eat.

equipment

6-hole (¾-cup/180ml) texas muffin pan
25cm-square prepared cake board
  (see *basic know-how number 2*,
    pages 160-161)

cake

470g packet buttercake mix
1 quantity butter cream (page 180)
green, pink and yellow food colouring

decorations

2 red sour straps, cut into thin strips
2 licorice allsorts
2 mini musk lollies, halved
2 x 40g jars BoPeep lollies
410g packet Smarties
3 fruit sticks

1 Preheat oven to 180°C/160°C fan-forced. Grease texas muffin pan.

2 Make cake according to directions on packet. Drop ⅓ cup of the mixture into each hole; bake about 25 minutes. Stand cakes in pan 5 minutes; turn, top-side up, onto wire rack to cool.

3 Divide butter cream equally into three small bowls; tint each bowl with one of the suggested colours: green, pink and yellow.

4 Level tops of all cakes. Using picture as a guide, spread the tops and sides of three cakes with one of the coloured butter creams. Position cakes on prepared board; secure with a little butter cream.

5 Using picture as a guide, trim remaining three cakes into roof shapes (see *step-by-step number 18*, page 169). Leave tops of the roofs flat. Spread roofs all over with butter cream; position roofs on the houses. Outline with strips of the sour straps.

6 Remove licorice layer from allsorts; trim the coloured layer into door shapes, place in position on houses. Secure mini musk halves to doors with a little butter cream for door knobs.

7 Position BoPeep lollies and Smarties for windows and roofs. Cut fruit sticks in half; position for chimneys.

Make a cottage for each year of the birthday child's age and, rather than using fruit sticks for the chimneys, use chunky coloured candles, instead.

cute cottages

tip You'll have about 1 cup of the cake mixture left over, enough to make another little house.

equipment

12-hole (⅓-cup/80ml) standard
  muffin pan
9-hole (½-cup/125ml) friand pan
45cm x 65cm prepared cake board
  (see *basic know-how number 2*,
  pages 160-161)

cake

1½ x 470g packets buttercake mix
1½ quantities butter cream (page 180)
green, orange and red food colouring

decorations

20cm x 15cm piece orange cardboard
30cm x 20cm piece yellow cardboard
8 after-dinner mints
200g milk chocolate Toblerone
300g packet mint leaves
4 red fruit rings
1 orange Smartie
1 brown Smartie
7cm piece black licorice strap
2 orange fruit rings
1 x 30cm (7mm) green chenille stick
  (pipe cleaner), cut into quarters

1 Preheat oven to 180°C/160°C fan-forced. Grease nine holes of the muffin pan; grease the friand pan.

2 Make cake according to directions on packets. Drop 2½ level tablespoons of the mixture into greased holes of the muffin pan; bake about 20 minutes. Stand cakes in pan 5 minutes; turn, top-side up, onto wire rack to cool.

This dragon is the perfect cake for a centrepiece; it can be made as long as you like by extending the tail. There is a pattern at the back of the book so you can make its fiery breath.

fiery dragon

3 Reduce oven temperature to 170°C/150°C fan-forced. Drop 2½ level tablespoons of the mixture into greased friand pan holes; bake about 20 minutes. Stand cakes in pan 5 minutes; turn, top-side up, onto wire rack to cool.

4 Tint two-thirds of the butter cream green. Divide remaining butter cream equally into two small bowls; tint one bowl orange and the other red.

5 Level friand tops. Use three friands to shape dragon's head (see *step-by-step number 19*, page 170). Spread green butter cream over tops and sides of each friand.

6 Level muffin tops. Turn eight muffins upside down; spread tops and sides of five muffins with orange butter cream; spread tops and sides of three muffins with red butter cream.

7 Trim the remaining muffin into a triangular shape for the tail; spread top and sides with red butter cream.

8 Using pattern sheet, from pattern sheet provided, cut out dragon's fiery breath from the yellow and orange cardboard. Position on prepared board. Using picture as a guide, position cakes on prepared board to make dragon. Position trimmed friands to make head; use the remaining six friands to make a triangular body. Use muffins to make neck and tail. Secure cakes with a little butter cream.

9 Using picture as a guide, cut after-dinner mints into triangles. Use triangular pieces and segments of Toblerone to decorate the dragon's body. Decorate dragon's head and body with mint leaves.

10 Use one red fruit ring to make the eye; top with an orange Smartie. Use brown Smartie for nose. Trim licorice strap to make mouth. Cut remaining red and orange fruit rings in half; use to decorate dragon's neck and tail.

11 Bend one end of each chenille stick to make dragon's legs and feet; position under body.

tip You'll have about ⅔ cup of the cake mixture left over. Make another four cakes for a longer tailed dragon, if you like.

butterfly cakes

A tiered cake plate is the perfect way to show off these ever-popular patty cakes. Make sure you have enough cakes for your guests.

equipment
3 x 12-hole (⅓-cup/80ml) standard
   muffin pans
30 standard paper cases

cake
2 x 470g packets buttercake mix
3¼ cups (500g) icing sugar
2 tablespoons water, approximately
pink and green food colouring
1 cup (80g) desiccated coconut
600ml thickened cream
2 tablespoons icing sugar, extra
⅓ cup (110g) strawberry jam

decorations
15 small pink jelly beans
15 pink ready-made icing flowers

1 Preheat oven to 180°C/160°C fan-forced. Line muffin pans with the paper cases.

2 Make cake according to directions on packets. Drop 2½ level tablespoons of the mixture into each paper case; bake about 20 minutes. Stand cakes in pans 5 minutes; turn, top-side up, onto wire rack to cool.

3 Sift half the icing sugar into a medium heatproof bowl; stir in enough water to make a stiff paste. Place bowl over medium saucepan of simmering water (do not let the water touch the bottom of the bowl); stir until icing is thin and spreadable. Tint with pink colouring.

4 Place coconut in a shallow bowl. Spread (or dip) the tops of half the cakes with icing; dip tops in coconut, stand cakes on wire rack to set.

5 Repeat step 3 with remaining icing sugar and water; tint with green colouring. Spread (or dip) the tops of remaining cakes with icing; dip tops in coconut, stand cakes on wire rack to set.

6 Meanwhile, beat cream and extra sifted icing sugar in small bowl with electric mixer until soft peaks form.

7 Cut 5mm-thick rounds from tops of all the cakes. Cut pink rounds in half to form butterfly "wings"; leave green rounds whole.

8 Drop ½ teaspoon jam into the hole in each cake; dollop with cream. Using picture as a guide, position "wings" on the pink cakes; top with jelly beans. Top green cakes with green rounds; secure flowers to cakes with a little cream.

tip You'll have about 1 cup of the cake mixture left over, enough for about six more little cakes.

fairy wings

Buy the birthday girl a doll she'll love then choose the colour for the wings to match the doll.

equipment
12-hole (2-tablespoons/40ml)
    deep flat-based patty pan
4 x 12-hole (1-tablespoon/20ml)
    mini muffin pans
10 standard paper cases (silver)
44 mini muffin paper cases (silver)
4.5cm-round fluted cutter
3cm-round fluted cutter
35cm x 45cm prepared cake board
    (see *basic know-how number 2,*
        pages 160-161)

cake
470g packet buttercake mix
¼ cup (80g) apricot jam,
    warmed, sieved
½ cup (80g) icing sugar
300g ready-made white icing
    (page 180)
pink food colouring

decorations
28cm doll
60g jar silver cachous
6 blue ready-made icing flowers
6 pink ready-made icing flowers

1 Preheat oven to 180°C/160°C fan-forced. Line patty pan with the standard paper cases. Line mini muffin pans with the mini paper cases.

2 Make cake according to directions on packet. Drop 2 level tablespoons of the mixture into each standard paper case; drop 2 level teaspoons of the mixture into each mini paper case. Bake large cakes about 20 minutes; bake small cakes about 15 minutes. Stand cakes in pans 5 minutes; turn, top-side up, onto wire rack to cool.

3 Brush tops of all cakes with jam. On a surface dusted with sifted icing sugar, knead the ready-made icing until smooth. Tint two-thirds of the icing pale pink; tint remaining icing dark pink (see *basic know-how number 16*, page 162).

4 Roll dark pink icing until 3mm thick. Cut 10 x 4.5cm rounds from icing; position rounds on large cakes. Roll pale pink icing until 3mm thick. Cut 44 x 3cm rounds from icing; position rounds on small cakes.

5 Position doll on prepared board. Using picture as a guide, position cakes around doll for wings; secure with a little butter cream. Gently push cachous onto pale pink cakes. Brush the backs of the ready-made icing flowers with a little water, then position on dark pink cakes.

equipment

12-hole (⅓-cup/80ml) standard
   muffin pan
2 x 12-hole (1-tablespoon/20ml)
   mini muffin pans
12-hole (2-tablespoons/40ml)
   deep flat-based patty pan
11 standard paper cases
   (7 green, 1 yellow, 3 brown)
24 mini muffin paper cases (2 purple,
   3 pink, 19 green)
50cm x 58cm prepared cake board
   (see *basic know-how number 2*,
      pages 160-161)

cake

470g packet buttercake mix
1 quantity butter cream (page 180)
green, brown, yellow, pink and purple
   food colouring

decorations

300g packet mint leaves
7 Jaffas, halved
1 pink fruit salad jelly,
   halved lengthways
hundreds and thousands
2cm piece musk stick, halved
6 yellow fruit rings, halved
410g packet Smarties
3cm red bootlace
4 foil-wrapped chocolate ladybirds
1 sour worm
150g packet rainbow choc-chips
1 giant white marshmallow
2 white marshmallows
3 white Mallow Bakes
1 pink mini musk
1cm piece black licorice strap,
   cut into thin strips

1 Preheat oven to 180°C/160°C
fan-forced. Line standard muffin pan
with the green and yellow standard
paper cases; line mini muffin pans with
the mini paper cases; line the patty
pan with brown standard paper cases.

2 Make cake according to directions
on packet. Drop 2½ level tablespoons
of the mixture into each paper case in
the standard muffin pan. Drop 2 level
tablespoons of the mixture into each
paper case in the patty pan. Bake
cakes about 20 minutes. Stand cakes
in pans 5 minutes; turn, top-side up,
onto wire rack to cool.

3 Drop 2 level teaspoons of the
mixture into the mini paper cases.
Bake about 15 minutes. Stand cakes
in pans 5 minutes; turn, top-side up,
onto wire rack to cool.

4 Design the garden on the board
using the cakes before icing them.

5 Divide butter cream into three small
bowls. Tint one bowl green and one
bowl dark green. Tint half the remaining
butter cream brown. Divide remaining
butter cream equally into three small
bowls. Tint each remaining bowl of
butter cream with one of the suggested
colours: yellow, pink and purple.

Arrange the cakes for your garden before you ice
them. Decorate them however you like, using
lollies and cute critters. Don't worry about the
scale of things, your guests won't mind at all.

magic garden

6 Spread brown butter cream over tops of tree trunk cakes; spread green butter cream over tops of the tree canopy cakes. Spread yellow butter cream over sun cake. Spread pink butter cream over the tops of three mini muffins in pink cases and purple butter cream over the tops of two mini muffins in purple cases; spread the remaining mini muffin cakes with dark green butter cream for garden bed.

7 Reserve three mint leaves; position remaining mint leaves and the Jaffa halves on tree canopy. Use a small sharp knife to cut the remaining mint leaves into thin strips; use to decorate the garden bed.

8 Sprinkle jelly halves with hundreds and thousands. Using picture as a guide, make butterfly by positioning jelly halves, cut-side up, on either side of musk stick half; place on tree.

9 Decorate sun with fruit ring halves; position red Smarties for eyes and red bootlace for the mouth.

10 Position ladybirds, brown Smarties for rocks, and sour worm in the garden.

11 Position pink and purple Smarties around same coloured cakes to make flower petals. Use yellow rainbow choc-chips to make the flower centres.

12 Use giant marshmallow for rabbit's body and smaller marshmallow for head. Cut remaining marshmallow in half; pinch slightly to shape into rabbit's ears. Position Mallow Bakes for feet and tail. Decorate rabbit's face with mini musk for nose, strips of licorice strap for whiskers and blue rainbow choc-chips for eyes; secure to face with a little butter cream.

Littlies

1

2

flower faces

These pretty cakes would look really good served on a cake stand – or on a long platter or cake board placed in the centre of the party table.

equipment
12-hole (⅓-cup/80ml) standard
   muffin pan
12 standard paper cases (white)

cake
470g packet buttercake mix
½ quantity butter cream (page 180)
yellow and purple food colouring

decorations
Each quantity of lollies is enough to
   make three flower faces.

gemma gerbera
15cm blue sugar-coated bootlace,
   cut into thirds
6 blue mini M&M's
24 small blue jelly beans

sunny sunflower
45 small yellow jelly beans
1½ teaspoons chocolate sprinkles
6 red mini M&M's
15cm red sugar-coated bootlace,
   cut into thirds

daisy daze
9 white marshmallows
6 pink mini musks
2 small red jelly beans,
   halved crossways
6cm red sugar-coated bootlace,
   cut into thirds

vicky violet
9 pink marshmallows
3 pink Mallow Bakes,
   halved crossways
6 mauve mini musks
2 small red jelly beans,
   halved lengthways

1 Preheat oven to 180°C/160°C
fan-forced. Line muffin pan with
the paper cases.

2 Make cake according to directions
on packet. Drop 2½ level tablespoons
of the mixture into each paper case;
bake about 20 minutes. Stand cakes in
pan 5 minutes; turn, top-side up, onto
wire rack to cool.

3 Place half the butter cream in a
small bowl; leave plain. Divide remaining
butter cream into two small bowls; tint
one bowl yellow and the other purple.

1 gemma gerbera

Spread half the plain butter cream over three cakes. Using picture as a guide, decorate cakes using the lollies listed at left.

2 sunny sunflower

Spread the remaining plain butter cream over three cakes. Using picture as a guide, decorate cakes using the lollies listed at left.

3 vicky violet

Spread purple butter cream over three cakes. Using scissors, cut marshmallows in half crossways; squeeze ends of each piece of marshmallow to make petals (see *basic know-how number 18*, page 163). Using picture as a guide, decorate cakes using the lollies listed at left.

4 daisy daze

Spread yellow butter cream over three cakes. Using scissors, cut marshmallows in half crossways; squeeze ends of each piece of marshmallow to make petals (see *basic know-how number 18*, page 163). Using picture as a guide, decorate cakes using the lollies listed at left.

tip You will have enough cake mixture left over to make about five more flower faces; you'll need more butter cream and decorations, though.

equipment
6-hole (¾-cup/180ml) texas muffin pan
5 texas muffin paper cases (yellow)

cake
470g packet buttercake mix
½ quantity butter cream (page 180)
blue, brown, pink, white and
yellow food colouring

decorations
pirate pete
8cm red sour strap
3 white Choc Bits
10cm black licorice strap,
cut into strips
1 green M&M
1 brown M&M
2 dark chocolate Melts

polar prince
2 brown Smarties
5cm black licorice strap,
cut into strips
2 white marshmallows

winnie
2 large pink candy hearts
hundreds and thousands
5 pink mini M&M's
1 orange mini M&M
2 red Smarties
5cm piece red sour strap,
cut into strips

betty blue
2 teaspoons blue sugar crystals (see
basic know-how number 25, page 164)
2 pink Smarties
1 small pink jelly bean
2 large yellow candy hearts
2 small yellow jelly beans
5 pink mini musks
2cm strip rainbow sour strap,
cut into strips

pink poppy
2 strawberries and cream lollies
2 purple Smarties
1 red sour strap, halved lengthways
2cm piece red licorice strap,
cut into strips

Make a teddy bear for each guest, maybe with
their names placed in front of each cake.

teddy bears

tips You will have enough cake mixture left over to make another four teddy bears. Place the cakes on a cake board, plate or platter.

1 Preheat oven to 180°C/160°C fan-forced. Line texas muffin pan with the paper cases.

2 Make cake according to directions on packet. Drop ⅓ cup of the mixture into each paper case; bake about 25 minutes. Stand cakes in pan 5 minutes; turn, top-side up, onto wire rack to cool.

3 Divide butter cream equally into five small bowls; tint each bowl with one of the suggested colours: blue, brown, pink, white and yellow.

1 pirate pete
Spread brown butter cream over top of cake. Using picture as a guide, decorate cake with the lollies listed at left.

2 polar prince
Spread white butter cream over top of cake. Using picture as a guide, decorate cake with the lollies listed at left.

3 winnie
Spread yellow butter cream over top of cake. Spread a little butter cream over each heart; sprinkle with hundreds and thousands. Using picture as a guide, decorate cake with the lollies listed at left.

4 betty blue
Spread blue butter cream over top of cake; sprinkle with blue sugar crystals. Using picture as a guide, decorate cake with lollies listed at left; secure with a little butter cream.

5 pink poppy
Spread pink butter cream over top of cake. Using picture as a guide, decorate cake with the lollies listed at left.

abc chart

We positioned each of the cakes in the chart on squares of paper and felt. This makes the cakes look like a proper chart, but it's not really necessary.

equipment

6-hole (¾-cup/180ml) texas muffin pan
12-hole (⅓-cup/80ml) standard
    muffin pan
12-hole (2-tablespoons/40ml)
    deep flat-based patty pan
3 texas muffin paper cases (blue)
6 standard paper cases (blue)
35cm-square prepared cake board
    (see *basic know-how number 2,*
        pages 160-161)

cake

470g packet buttercake mix
½ quantity butter cream (page 180)
blue and white food colouring

decorations

¼ cup (40g) icing sugar
100g ready-made white icing
    (page 180)

1 Preheat oven to 180°C/160°C fan-forced. Line three holes of the texas muffin pan with texas paper cases; line three holes of the standard muffin pan with standard paper cases; line three holes of the patty pan with standard paper cases.

2 Make cake according to directions on packet. Drop ⅓ cup of the mixture into each texas paper case. Bake about 25 minutes. Drop 2½ level tablespoons of the mixture into each paper case in the standard muffin pan. Drop 2 level tablespoons of the mixture into each paper case in the patty pan. Bake cakes about 20 minutes. Stand cakes in pans 5 minutes; turn, top-side up, onto wire rack to cool.

3 Divide butter cream equally into two small bowls; tint one light blue and the other white.

4 Using picture as a guide, spread blue and white butter cream over the tops of the cakes. Position on board; secure with a little butter cream.

5 On a surface dusted with sifted icing sugar, knead the ready-made icing until smooth. Divide icing into two equal portions; tint one portion blue; leave the other portion white (see *basic know-how number 16,* page 162). Roll each portion out to 3mm thickness. Using paper pattern, from pattern sheet provided, cut out shapes and letters for the cakes from the icings (see *basic know-how number 17,* pages 162-163). Using picture as a guide, position shapes and letters on cakes.

milly mouse

equipment

2 x 12-hole (1-tablespoon/20ml)
   mini muffin pans
8-hole (½-cup/125ml) mini loaf pan
9-hole (½-cup/125ml) friand pan
18 mini muffin paper cases (white)
35cm x 45cm prepared cake board
   (see *basic know-how number 2*,
   pages 160-161)

cake

½ x 470g packet buttercake mix
½ quantity butter cream (page 180)
pink, orange and yellow
   food colouring

decorations

½ cup (40g) desiccated coconut
2 x 8cm black licorice rope,
   halved lengthways
16cm piece black licorice strap
1 pink marshmallow
1 pink Mallow Bake
1 brown M&M
85g packet pink jelly crystals
85g packet orange jelly crystals
85g packet yellow jelly crystals
ribbon

1 Preheat oven to 170°C/150°C fan-forced. Line the mini muffin pans with paper cases. Grease one hole of the loaf pan; grease one hole of the friand pan.

2 Make cake according to directions on packet. Drop 2 level teaspoons of the mixture into the paper cases; bake about 15 minutes. Drop ¼ cup of the mixture into the greased hole of the friand pan. Drop ⅓ cup of the mixture into the greased hole of the loaf pan. Bake cakes about 25 minutes. Stand cakes in pans 5 minutes; turn, top-side up, onto wire rack to cool.

3 Divide half the butter cream equally into three small bowls; tint each with one of the suggested colours: pink, orange and yellow. Keep remaining butter cream plain.

4 Using a small serrated knife, cut the loaf cake into an oval shape for the mouse's body; trim friand cake into a rounded shape for mouse's head. Spread plain butter cream over top and sides of the body and head; roll cakes in coconut. Position mouse's head and body on prepared board; secure with a little butter cream.

5 Cut 7cm, 5cm, 4cm and 2cm lengths from licorice halves; use fingers to shape 7cm and 5cm lengths of licorice into mouse's legs. Using picture as a guide, position legs. Use fingers to shape 4cm and 2cm lengths of licorice to make mouse's arms; position on the cake. Secure all with a little butter cream.

6 Cut licorice strap in half lengthways, then in half lengthways again (you will have 4 lengths of strap); position one length for mouse's tail. Trim remaining pieces to size and position for whiskers and mouth. Split marshmallow in half; position for ear. Position Mallow Bake for nose and M&M for eye.

7 Spread tops of six mini muffins with the pink butter cream; spread tops of six mini muffins with orange butter cream and spread remaining mini muffins with yellow butter cream. Sprinkle with matching jelly crystals; position on board; secure with a little butter cream. Cut and position lengths of ribbon for balloon strings.

good ship

We used calico for the sail, and a scrap of ribbon for the patch. The flag was made from paper and a toothpick. They were attached to the bread-stick mast with tiny strips of gaffer tape.

equipment

20cm x 30cm lamington pan
5 x 12-hole (1-tablespoon/20ml)
   mini muffin pans
57 mini paper cases (3 red, 54 green)
40cm x 55cm prepared cake board (see
   basic know-how number 2,
      pages 160-161)

cake

2 x 470g packets buttercake mix
1 quantity butter cream (pages 180)
green food colouring

decorations

2 x 140g packets Monster 5s
3 red fruit rings
180g packet Smarties
1 small yellow lollipop
1 grissini bread stick
20cm-square unbleached calico
1 cat-shaped soft toy
15cm x 10cm piece brown cardboard
1 mini muffin paper case (brown)
5cm x 5cm piece white cardboard

1 Preheat oven to 180°C/160°C fan-forced. Grease lamington pan; line base and sides with baking paper, extending paper 5cm over long sides. Line muffin pans with the paper cases.

2 Make one cake according to directions on packet. Spread mixture into lamington pan; bake about 35 minutes. Stand cake in pan 5 minutes; turn, top-side up, onto wire rack to cool.

3 Make remaining cake. Drop 2 level teaspoons of the mixture into each paper case; bake about 15 minutes. Stand cakes in pans 5 minutes; turn, top-side up, onto wire rack to cool.

4 Level top of large cake. Turn cake cut-side down; using paper pattern, from pattern sheet provided, cut ship from cake. Trim cake to make a curved hull (see *step-by-step number 20*, pages 170-171). Position ship on board, cut-side down; secure with a little butter cream, discard remaining cake.

5 Reserve 1 tablespoon of the butter cream. Tint remaining butter cream green. Spread two-thirds of the butter cream all over ship; spread remaining butter cream over tops of small cakes in green cases. Sprinkle green hundreds and thousands over cakes. Spread plain butter cream over cakes in red cases.

6 Using picture as a guide, position red cakes in centre of the ship to resemble port holes; top each with a red fruit ring and a red Smartie.

7 Decorate ship with rows of green cakes. Using picture as a guide, position lollipop and Smarties on ship; secure with a little butter cream.

8 Use the bread stick for the mast; position the sail, flags and cat.

9 Using picture as a guide, make owl. Cut a 7cm and 4.5cm circle from cardboard. Shape and cut owl's ears from top of smaller circle; tape "head" to larger circle. Flatten mini paper case; cut a small triangular piece from paper case about 4.5cm across, tape to back of owl's head for feathers. Fold paper case so it fits to front of owl for feathers; glue into position. Cut two 2cm circles from white cardboard for eyes, draw on owl's eyes; glue into position. Use gaffer tape to make and position owl's feet and beak. Position owl on boat.

tips We used two pieces of cardboard of the owl, brown for the head and yellow for body, however, a single colour will look just as good.

You'll have about 1 cup of the cake mixture left over, enough for about 24 mini cakes. The cake mixture will be fine standing at room temperature if you have to bake the cakes in batches.

equipment

8-hole (½-cup/125ml) mini loaf pan
30cm x 60cm prepared cake board
    (see *basic know-how number 2*,
    pages 160-161)

cake

470g packet buttercake mix
1 quantity butter cream (page 180)
green and yellow food colouring

decorations

1 green fruit stick, cut into thirds
1 yellow fruit stick, cut into thirds
4 yellow fruit rings
1 black licorice strap
2 chocolate cream biscuits
9 mini chocolate cream biscuits,
    split in half
350g packet jubes
225g packet jelly beans
340g packet Smarties

1 Preheat oven to 170°C/150°C fan-forced. Grease six holes of the mini loaf pan.

2 Make cake according to directions on packet. Drop ⅓ cup of the mixture into greased holes; bake about 25 minutes. Stand cakes in pan 5 minutes; turn, top-side up, onto wire rack to cool.

3 Transfer a third of the butter cream to a small bowl; tint green. Tint remaining butter cream yellow.

4 Level tops of cakes so they are the same height. Using picture as a guide, position two of the cakes in an L-shape to make the engine; secure with a little butter cream. Position on prepared board. Spread engine cakes with green butter cream.

5 Spread the carriages with yellow butter cream; position on the board, secure with a little butter cream. Use pieces of fruit stick between the engine and the carriages.

6 Position fruit rings for the smoke stack. Cut two 1.5cm squares from the licorice strap; use for windows. Cut remaining licorice strap into thin strips; use strips to outline engine and tops of carriages.

7 Use biscuits for wheels. Top carriages with jubes, jelly beans and Smarties.

tips You will have enough cake mixture left over to make four more carriages, if you like. Push a wooden skewer through the fruit ring smoke stack and into the cake, then attach some cotton wool for smoke.

choo choo train

fishbowl fun

equipment

12-hole (1-tablespoon/20ml)
   mini muffin pan
deep 30cm-round cake pan
35cm-square prepared cake board
   (see *basic know-how number 2*,
   pages 160-161)

cake

2 x 470g packets buttercake mix
1½ quantities butter cream (page 180)
blue, white, pink and yellow
   food colouring

decorations

pink sprinkles
yellow sprinkles
3 yellow triangular jubes,
   halved lengthways
2 red triangular jubes,
   halved lengthways
18 blue mini M&M's
150g packet rainbow choc-chips
10cm red sugar-coated bootlace
200g packet small jelly beans
4 mint leaves, cut into thin strips
1 x 15g Flake bar, broken into pieces

1 Preheat oven to 180°C/160°C fan-forced. Grease five holes of the mini muffin pan; grease and line round cake pan (see *basic know-how numbers 3-6*, pages 160-161)

2 Make cake according to directions on packets. Drop 3 level teaspoons of the mixture into the greased mini muffin holes; bake about 15 minutes. Spread remaining mixture into round cake pan; bake about 40 minutes. Stand cakes in pans 5 minutes; turn, top-side up, onto wire rack to cool.

3 Level top of large cake; turn cake cut-side down. Using paper pattern, from pattern sheet provided, cut fishbowl from cake; position on prepared board, secure with a little butter cream.

4 Place two-thirds of the butter cream in a small bowl; tint blue. Place half the remaining butter cream in a small bowl; tint white. Place half the remaining butter cream in a small bowl; tint pink, tint remaining butter cream yellow.

5 Using picture as a guide, spread the blue butter cream over the top and sides of about three quarters of the cake to make water. Spread plain butter cream over the top of the cake (see *step-by-step number 21*, page 171).

6 Spread pink butter cream all over top and sides of two mini muffins; spread yellow butter cream all over top and sides of remaining cakes. Place pink and yellow sprinkles in separate small shallow bowls. Roll sides of pink muffins in pink sprinkles, roll sides of yellow muffins in yellow sprinkles; position on fishbowl. Trim jubes to resemble fins and tails. Using matching colours, position jubes on cakes for fins and tails.

7 Using picture as a guide, use mini M&M's for bubbles. Decorate fish with rainbow choc-chips; use blue rainbow choc-chips for eyes. Use strips of red bootlace for mouths.

8 Decorate fish bowl with jelly beans, strips of mint leaves and pieces of Flake.

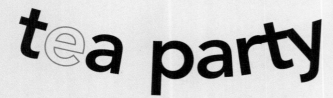 t(e)a party

Little girls love tea parties – the whole party could be themed this way. The cakes are not difficult to make, but they are quite time-consuming.

equipment
12-hole (1-tablespoon/20ml) shallow round-based patty pan
12-hole (⅓-cup/80ml) standard muffin pan
6-hole (¾-cup/180ml) texas muffin pan
4cm-round cutter
2 strong wooden toothpicks
40cm-round or 40cm x 45cm rectangle prepared cake board (see *basic know-how numbers 1-2*, pages 160-161)

cake
470g packet buttercake mix
2 quantities butter cream (page 180)
pink and green food colouring

decorations
5 x giant freckles
1 small red fruit ring, halved
3 small green fruit rings, halved
1 large green fruit ring
9 small green ready-made icing hearts
1 tablespoon demerara sugar, optional

1 Preheat oven to 180°C/160°C fan-forced. Grease one hole of the patty pan; grease five holes of the standard muffin pan; grease one hole of the texas muffin pan.

2 Make cake according to directions on packet. Drop 3 level teaspoons of the mixture into the greased patty pan hole; bake about 10 minutes. Drop 2½ level tablespoons of the mixture into the greased standard muffin pan holes; drop ⅓ cup of the mixture into the greased texas muffin pan hole; bake cakes about 20 minutes. Stand cakes in pans 5 minutes; turn, top-side up, onto wire rack to cool.

3 Divide butter cream equally between two small bowls; tint one bowl pink and the other green.

4 Level cake tops. Using picture as a guide, trim the five standard muffin cakes to make teacup shapes. Using a 4cm-round cutter, mark circles on the five teacup shapes. Scoop out cake from the cups, making 4cm-deep hollows (see *step-by-step number 22*, page 170). Trim texas muffin cake to make teapot shape.

5 Turn giant freckles upside-down; spread the bases with pink or green butter cream to make saucers. Position on prepared board; secure with a little butter cream.

6 Spread the teacups, inside and out, with pink or green butter cream; position on saucers. Position small fruit rings on teacups for handles.

7 Spread green butter cream all over teapot. Position on prepared board; secure with a little butter cream. Spread pink butter cream over rounded bottom of patty cake; position on teapot for lid, top with a small fruit ring half. Cut large fruit ring in half; shape end and position for the teapot handle and spout, secure to teapot with toothpicks. Decorate lid with icing hearts. Sprinkle 2 teaspoons of the sugar into two of the cups to resemble tea, if you like.

tips Add the demerara sugar (or raw sugar would do) just before the start of the party. If you freeze the cut pieces of cake for an hour or so, it will help minimise the cake crumbling.

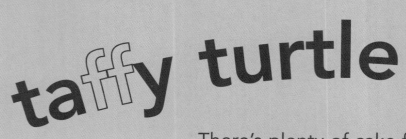

taffy turtle

There's plenty of cake for all the guests in this jigsaw-patterned turtle. We made the watery waves from pieces of felt, although paper would do just as well.

equipment

6-hole (¾-cup/180ml) texas muffin pan
8-hole (½-cup/125ml) mini loaf pan
2.25-litre (9-cup) pudding steamer
45cm-square prepared cake board
  (see *basic know-how number 2*,
  pages 160-161)

cake

2 x 470g packets buttercake mix
3 quantities butter cream (page 180)
green and orange food colouring

decorations

3 yellow fruit rings, halved
22 orange fruit rings
33 green M&M's
28 blue mini M&M's
6 blue M&M's
2 round peppermints
4cm strip red bootlace

1 Preheat oven to 170°C/150°C fan-forced. Grease one hole of the texas muffin pan; grease five holes of the loaf pan. Grease the pudding steamer.

2 Drop ⅓ cup of the mixture into the greased texas muffin pan hole; drop ⅓ cup of the mixture into the greased loaf pan holes. Bake about 25 minutes. Stand cakes in pans 5 minutes; turn, top-side up, onto wire rack to cool.

3 Pour remaining mixture into pudding steamer; bake about 1 hour. Stand cake in pan 5 minutes; turn onto wire rack to cool.

4 Turn pudding cake top-side up; level top, turn cut-side down. Using paper pattern, from pattern sheet provided, cut the hexagon shape from the centre of the pudding cake (see *step-by-step number 23*, pages 170-171). Using picture as a guide, cut through the cake from each point of the hexagon.

5 Shape muffin into a rounded shape for head (see *step-by-step number 3*, page 167). Using paper pattern, cut two small and two large flippers from four of the loaf cakes (see *step-by-step number 24*, page 171). Shape tail from remaining loaf cake.

6 Tint three-quarters of the butter cream green; tint remaining butter cream orange. Using picture as a guide, assemble the cake, one piece at a time, from the hexagon centre outwards; secure pieces to prepared board with a little butter cream as you go. Spread green butter cream over the tops and sides of the body pieces. Spread orange butter cream over top and sides of turtle's head, tail and flippers.

7 Using picture as a guide, use decorations for the turtle's shell, flippers and tail. Secure a blue M&M onto each peppermint with a little butter cream; position on head for eyes. Shape and position red bootlace for turtle's mouth.

equipment

30cm x 45cm prepared cake board
(see *basic know-how number 2*,
    pages 160-161)
strong wooden toothpick

cake

450g packet chocolate lamingtons
    (six in each packet)
350g packet lamington fingers
    (18 in each packet)
½ quantity butter cream (page 180)

humpty dumptys

2 medium Easter eggs
2 x 30cm (3mm) yellow chenille sticks
    (pipe cleaners)
red decorating gel
4 blue mini M&M's

2 red mini muffin paper cases
2 freckles
1 round red jube, cut in half

decorations

27 Maltesers, approximately
2 green snakes, halved lengthways
5 mint leaves
3 yellow ready-made icing flowers
3 foil-wrapped chocolate ladybirds

1 Cut large lamingtons in half
crossways. Using picture as a guide,
assemble large lamingtons in two
layers to make base and sides of
wall on the prepared board; make
one side a little shorter than the other,
and position lamingtons in "steps" at
sides. Use butter cream to "cement"
lamingtons in place.

2 Top wall and sides with lamington
fingers to give 3 layers, cementing
each with butter cream. Make the
steps in front of the wall using three
lamington fingers.

3 Use a toothpick to gently make holes in the eggs for arms and legs. Cut one chenille stick into four pieces: two shorter lengths for the arms and two longer lengths for the legs. Gently push chenille sticks into the holes for the arms and legs. Use red decorating gel to make Humpty's mouth; use red decorating gel to secure two blue mini M&M's for eyes.

4 Make hats from the paper cases; secure freckles and jube halves to the top of the hats with a little butter cream.

5 Secure Maltesers to board with a little butter cream. Using picture as a guide, decorate the wall with remaining decorations. Position both Humptys as you like.

tip If Easter eggs aren't available, you can use Kinder Surprise eggs.

tumbledown humpty

We've made quite a long wall out of bought lamingtons; you could have quite a few Humptys in various stages of falling off the wall, if you like.

flower jigsaw

The hardest part of making this cake is making the butter cream smooth on the sides of the petals where the cake has been cut. If you freeze the cut cake pieces for an hour or so, it will help minimise the cake crumbling.

equipment
deep 30cm-round cake pan
40cm-square prepared cake board
   (see *basic know-how number 2*,
      pages 160-161)

cake
2 x 470g packets buttercake mix
2½ quantities butter cream (page 180)
yellow and orange food colouring

decorations
200g packet mini M&M's

1 Preheat oven to 180°C/160°C fan-forced. Grease and line round cake pan (see *basic know-how numbers 3-6*, pages 160-161).

2 Make cake according to directions on packets. Spread mixture into pan; bake about 1 hour. Stand cake in pan 5 minutes; turn, top-side up, onto wire rack to cool.

3 Level cake top; turn cake cut-side down. Using paper pattern, from pattern sheet provided, cut flower petals and centre from cake.

4 Place half the butter cream in a small bowl; tint yellow. Tint remaining butter cream orange.

5 Using picture as a guide, spread yellow butter cream all over tops and sides of flower centre and three of the petals; place on prepared board, secure with a little butter cream. Decorate with yellow mini M&M's.

6 Spread orange butter cream all over tops and sides of remaining petals. Decorate with orange mini M&M's.

blocks

The blocks are not difficult to make, but they are time-consuming to ice, especially if you want them to be perfect. The guests won't notice any rough edges, though.

equipment
deep 19cm-square cake pan
35cm x 45cm prepared cake board
  (see *basic know-how number 2*,
    pages 160-161)

cake
2 x 470g packets buttercake mix
1 quantity fluffy mock cream frosting
  (page 180)
pink, yellow and green food colouring

decorations
160g packet red sour straps
2 x 35g tubes mini M&M's
18 freckles, halved

1 Preheat oven to 180°C/160°C fan-forced. Grease and line cake pan (see *basic know-how number 7*, page 160), extending paper 5cm over sides.

2 Make cake according to directions on packets. Spread mixture into pan; bake about 50 minutes. Stand cake in pan 5 minutes; turn, top-side up, onto wire rack to cool.

3 Level top of cake; cut cake into nine cubes (see tip, page 90).

4 Divide fluffy mock cream frosting into four small bowls; leave one bowl plain, tint each remaining bowl with one of the suggested colours: pink, yellow and green. Spread frostings over the top and sides of cubes.

5 Cut sour straps into thin strips. Use to outline the sides of each cube.

6 Using picture as a guide, decorate cubes with butterflies, numbers and boats made from lollies listed at left.

7 Using a large palette knife, or egg slide, position and stack cubes on the prepared board.

paint pots

Parties for budding artists are popular – this cake will get them in the creative mood. Lollies could easily be hidden under the glacé icing.

equipment
6-hole (¾-cup/180ml) texas muffin pan
6cm-round cutter
30cm x 40cm prepared cake board
  (see *basic know-how number 2*,
  pages 160-161)

cake
470g packet buttercake mix
½ quantity butter cream (page 180)
1½ quantities glacé icing (page 180)
black, orange, blue, yellow, green
  and red food colouring

decorations
3 clean new paint brushes

1 Preheat oven to 180°C/160°C fan-forced. Grease texas muffin pan.

2 Make cake according to directions on packet. Drop ⅓ cup of the mixture into each hole; bake about 25 minutes. Stand cakes in pan 5 minutes; turn, top-side up, onto wire rack to cool.

3 Level cake tops so they are the same height. Using a 6cm-round cutter, make an imprint in the top of each cake; scoop out cake to make a 1.5cm-deep hollow in each cake (see *step-by-step number 22*, page 170).

4 Tint butter cream black; spread all over the side and top edge of each cake. Position cakes on board; secure with a little butter cream.

5 Divide glacé icing into five small bowls. Tint each bowl with one of the suggested colours: red, yellow, green, orange and blue.

6 Fill the hollow in each cake with one of the coloured icings. Position brushes as you like.

tips The cutter we used was about 5cm deep, which made it easier to cut right through the cake. You could use a sharp pointed vegetable knife to cut out the cake rounds, cutting around the markings of the shorter cutter. Freeze the little round cakes first for about an hour to help prevent them from crumbling while icing.

equipment

deep 30cm-round cake pan
3cm-round cutter
40cm-square prepared cake board
    (see *basic know-how number 2*,
        pages 160-161)

cake

1½ x 470g packets buttercake mix
1½ quantities butter cream (page 180)
yellow food colouring

decorations

hundreds & thousands
18 freckles
ribbon

1 Preheat oven to 180°C/160°C fan-forced. Grease and line cake pan (see *basic know-how numbers 3-6*, pages 160-161).

2 Make cake according to directions on packets. Spread mixture into pan; bake about 45 minutes. Stand cake in pan 5 minutes; turn, top-side up, onto wire rack to cool.

3 Level cake top; turn cake cut-side down. Using paper pattern, from pattern sheet provided, cut top of umbrella from cake (see *step-by-step number 25*, page 170). Position on prepared board; secure with a little butter cream. Reserve remaining cake.

4 Cut eight 3cm rounds from the reserved cake to make the umbrella's handle (see *step-by-step number 26*, pages 170-171).

5 Tint butter cream yellow; spread all over the top, sides and scallops of the umbrella.

6 Working with one round of cake at a time, spread butter cream over the top and side of each round; roll the side in hundreds and thousands (see *basic know-how number 27*, page 165). Position on the board; secure with a little butter cream; top with a freckle.

7 Decorate the top of the umbrella with remaining freckles and a bow.

sunny umbrella

ice-cream cones

These ice-cream look-alikes will dazzle the party guests. Make one for each guest or arrange them on a long platter or board. Let your imagination fly with different colours, toppings and decorations.

equipment
6-hole (¾-cup/180ml) texas muffin pan

cake
470g packet buttercake mix
1 quantity butter cream (page 180)
1 tablespoon cocoa powder
pink food colouring
6 square-based ice-cream cones

tip You will have enough cake mixture left over to make four more ice-cream cones if you like. Be careful handling the cones as they are a little top-heavy.

decorations

hundreds and thousands
choc sprinkles
2 red glacé cherries
40g dark chocolate Melts, melted
1 teaspoon crushed unsalted peanuts
1 ice-cream wafer
5 white Choc Bits
1 wafer stick, halved

1 Preheat oven to 180°C/160°C fan-forced. Grease texas muffin pan.

2 Make cake according to directions on packet. Drop ⅓ cup of the mixture into each hole; bake about 25 minutes. Stand cakes in pan 5 minutes; turn, top-side up, onto wire rack to cool.

3 Trim tops of cakes to make them a dome shape (see *step-by-step number 35*, pages 172-173).

4 Divide butter cream into three small bowls. Leave one bowl plain; stir sifted cocoa into another bowl. Tint remaining butter cream pink.

5 Using picture as a guide, spread the cakes with the different coloured butter creams.

6 Top each ice-cream cone with a cake. Using picture as a guide, decorate the cones using decorations listed at left.

tip To toast the coconut, put it in a large frying pan, then stir it constantly over a medium heat until it is browned lightly and evenly. Immediately turn the coconut out of the pan and spread it onto a large tray to cool it as fast as possible.

sandcastle

equipment

deep 19cm-square cake pan
8-hole (½-cup/125ml) mini loaf pan
6-hole (¾-cup/180ml) texas muffin pan
12-hole (⅓-cup/80ml) standard
   muffin pan
12-hole (1-tablespoon/20ml)
   mini-muffin pan
30cm-square prepared cake board
   (see *basic know-how number 2*,
     pages 160-161)

cake

2 x 470g packets buttercake mix
1½ quantities butter cream (page 180)
yellow food colouring
2 cups (160g) desiccated coconut,
   toasted (see tip, left)

decorations

4 round jubes
4 oval jubes
17 small purple jelly beans,
   halved crossways
2 small orange jelly beans,
   halved crossways
2 round green lollipops
1 sour worm
2 fruit rings
8 chocolate seahorses or shells
   (see tip, right)
1 foil-wrapped chocolate fish
paper flags

1 Preheat oven to 170°C/150°C fan-forced. Grease square cake pan; line base and sides with baking paper, extending paper 5cm over sides (see *basic know-how number 7*, page 160). Grease two holes of the loaf pan and one hole of the texas muffin pan. Grease four holes of the standard muffin pan and nine holes of the mini muffin pan.

2 Make cake according to directions on packets. Drop ¼ cup of the mixture into the greased holes of the loaf pan; drop ⅓ cup of the mixture into the greased hole of the texas muffin pan. Bake cakes about 25 minutes. Stand cakes in pans 5 minutes; turn, top-side up, onto wire rack to cool.

3 Drop 2½ level tablespoons of the mixture into the greased holes of the standard muffin pan. Bake cakes about 20 minutes. Drop 2 level teaspoons of the mixture into the greased holes of the mini muffin pan. Bake cakes about 15 minutes. Stand cakes in pans 5 minutes; turn, top-side up, onto wire rack to cool.

4 Spread remaining mixture into square pan. Bake about 50 minutes. Stand cake in pan 5 minutes; turn, top-side up, onto wire rack to cool.

5 Level all cake tops. Place square cake, cut-side down, on prepared board; secure with a little butter cream. Tint butter cream pale yellow; spread butter cream over top and sides of the large cake. Sprinkle all over with the coconut, pressing into sides of cake.

6 Spread small cakes, one at a time, all over with butter cream then roll to cover in the coconut.

7 Assemble sandcastle by positioning four standard muffins in centre of the square cake; top with loaf cakes then top with texas muffin.

8 Position mini muffins on top of the castle and around the edge of the square cake to make turrets.

9 Using picture as a guide, position the decorations on the castle, securing with a little butter cream when necessary.

tip We made our own white chocolate seahorses and shells using 100g melted white chocolate Melts in chocolate moulds. However, you can readily buy marbled white and milk chocolate seahorses or shells.

tip You'll have about 1 cup of the cake mixture left over; use it to make extra small cakes for the party.

ferris wheel

Place this large cake on a small table covered with greaseproof blue plastic (or something that will tolerate the grease from the butter cream), and use cotton wool to make some fluffy clouds.

equipment

6-hole (¾-cup/180ml) texas muffin pan
2 x 12-hole (1-tablespoon/20ml) mini muffin pans
15 mini muffin paper cases (red)
40cm x 50cm prepared cake board (see *basic know-how number 2*, pages 160-161)

cake

470g packet buttercake mix
1 quantity butter cream (page 180)
pink, green, yellow, purple and orange food colouring

decorations

40cm black licorice strap
250g packet musk sticks
1 pink Smartie
4 red sour straps
35g tube mini M&M's
35g jar small ready-made icing hearts
40g jar BoPeep lollies
1 licorice allsort
red decorating gel

1 Preheat oven to 180°C/160°C fan-forced. Grease four holes of the texas muffin pan. Line mini muffin pans with the paper cases.

2 Make cake according to directions on packet. Drop ⅓ cup of the mixture into greased holes of the texas muffin pan; bake about 25 minutes. Drop 2 level teaspoons of the mixture into each mini paper case; bake about 15 minutes. Stand cakes in pans 5 minutes; turn, top-side up, onto wire rack to cool.

3 Place a quarter of the butter cream in a small bowl; tint pink. Divide remaining butter cream equally into four small bowls; tint each with one of the suggested colours: green, yellow, purple and orange.

4 Spread pink butter cream over tops of small cakes. Position licorice strap at the bottom of the prepared board for road; secure with a little butter cream.

5 Using picture as a guide, make the base for the ferris wheel with 14 small cakes; secure with a little butter cream. Cut a musk stick in half: use the halves as supports for the wheel. Position the remaining small cake for the centre of the wheel; top with Smartie. Position eight musk sticks for the spokes of the wheel.

6 To make the carriages, cut the large cakes in half crossways. Using picture as a guide, spread tops and sides of cakes with the coloured butter creams. Position cakes on the board; secure with a little butter cream. Use trimmed musk sticks to complete the wheel.

7 Using picture as a guide, decorate the carriages with trimmed pieces of sour straps, mini M&M's, little hearts, BoPeep lollies and strips cut from the coloured layers of the licorice allsort. Secure lollies with tiny dabs of butter cream. Number the carriages using the decorating gel.

games

balls

equipment
6-hole (¾-cup/180ml) texas muffin pan
6 texas muffin paper cases (brown)

cake
470g packet buttercake mix
½ quantity butter cream (page 180)

decorations
soccer ball
white food colouring
1 black licorice strap

basketball
orange food colouring
black decorating gel

baseball
white food colouring
red decorating gel

tennis ball
yellow food colouring
85g packet yellow jelly crystals
white decorating gel

snooker ball
green food colouring
2 tablespoons icing sugar
50g ready-made white icing
  (page 180)
4.5cm-round cutter
black decorating gel

cricket ball
red food colouring
white decorating gel

1 Preheat oven to 180°C/160°C fan-forced. Line texas muffin pan with the paper cases.

2 Make cake according to directions on packet. Drop ⅓ cup of the mixture into each paper case; bake about 25 minutes. Stand cakes in pan 5 minutes; turn, top-side up, onto wire rack to cool.

tip The quantities we've given are enough to make six of any one type of ball, but there is enough cake mixture to make another three balls.

1 soccer ball

Tint butter cream with white colouring; spread over cake tops. Using paper pattern, from pattern sheet provided, cut 6 five-sided shapes and 30 small triangles from licorice. Using picture as a guide, position flat licorice pieces on cakes. Cut licorice into small strips, long enough to join flat licorice pieces.

2 basketball

Tint butter cream with orange colouring; spread over cake tops. Using picture as a guide, use black decorating gel to mark lines on cakes.

3 baseball

Tint butter cream with white colouring; spread over cake tops. Using picture as a guide, use red decorating gel to make dotted lines on the cakes.

4 tennis ball

Tint butter cream with yellow colouring; spread over cake tops, sprinkle with jelly crystals. Using picture as a guide, use white decorating gel to mark lines on the cakes.

5 snooker ball

Tint butter cream with green colouring; spread over cake tops. On a surface dusted with sifted icing sugar, knead the ready-made icing until smooth. Roll icing until 3mm thick, cut into six 4.5cm rounds; position on cakes. Use black decorating gel to write numbers on the icing.

6 cricket ball

Tint butter cream with red colouring; spread over cake tops. Using picture as a guide, use white decorating gel to make a series of six broken lines down the centre of the cakes.

tip Make a yo-yo for each guest; stack them in a bowl or basket etc., on the party table. If you like, join the yo-yos with a little jam as well as the butter cream.

yo-yos

equipment

2 x 12-hole (1-tablespoon/20ml)
  shallow round-based patty pans
6cm-round cutter

cake

½ x 470g packet buttercake mix
¼ quantity butter cream (page 180)
red, yellow and blue food colouring
¼ cup (80g) apricot jam,
  warmed, sieved
½ cup (80g) icing sugar
500g ready-made white icing
  (page 180)

decorations

100g packet black licorice bootlace,
  cut into 12 x 1m lengths

1 Preheat oven to 180°C/160°C fan-forced. Grease patty pans.

2 Make cake according to directions on packet. Drop 3 level teaspoons of mixture into each pan hole; bake about 10 minutes. Stand cakes in pans 5 minutes; turn onto wire rack to cool.

3 Divide butter cream into three small bowls; tint each bowl with one of the suggested colours: red, blue and yellow.

4 Brush warm jam over rounded bottoms of cakes. On a surface dusted with sifted icing sugar, knead the ready-made icing until smooth. Divide icing into three equal portions; tint each portion with one of the suggested colours: red, yellow and blue (see *basic know-how number 16*, page 162). Roll each portion into a 3mm thickness. Cut eight 6cm rounds from each portion.

5 Using picture as a guide, and using hands dusted with icing sugar, gently mould, shape and smooth the icing over the bottom of one cake at a time; fold a little icing over flat edge to cover edges (see *step-by-step number 27*, page 171). Repeat with remaining cakes and icing. Stand cakes, rounded-side up, on a fine wire rack for about 30 minutes or until the icing is firm. Sandwich cakes with a little butter cream. Wrap lengths of bootlace around each yo-yo.

dominoes

equipment
2 x 8cm x 26cm bar cake pans
35cm x 50cm prepared cake board
(see *basic know-how number 2*,
pages 160-161)

cake
½ x 470g packet buttercake mix
½ quantity butter cream (page 180)
white food colouring

decorations
6cm black licorice strap,
cut into thin strips
2 x 35g tubes mini M&M's

1 Preheat oven to 180°C/160°C fan-forced. Grease bar cake pans; line base and long sides with baking paper, extending paper 5cm over sides.

2 Make cake according to directions on packet. Drop ⅔ cup of the mixture into each pan; bake about 35 minutes. Stand cakes in pans 5 minutes; turn, top-side up, onto wire rack to cool.

3 Stir a little white colouring into butter cream to make it as white as possible. Spread butter cream over tops of cakes; cut each cake crossways into eight 3cm-wide pieces.

4 Cut strips of licorice strap into 16 x 3cm pieces. Position cakes on board; secure with a little butter cream. Using picture as a guide, position licorice strips on each piece of cake; decorate with mini M&M's.

> **tip** Use only ⅔ cup of the cake mixture in each cake pan; the cakes must be shallow and flat on top. You will only have a tiny amount of mixture left over. You can make up to 24 dominoes from the two bar cakes.

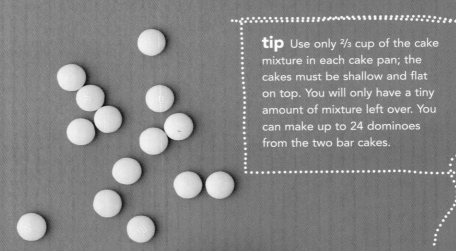

musical notes

Encourage the guests to bring their instruments, if possible, to a musically-themed party. A white board would make a perfect background for this cake; use a black marker to draw the lines.

equipment
2 x 12-hole (2-tablespoons/40ml)
   deep flat-based patty pans
24 standard paper cases (brown)
40cm-square prepared cake board
   (see *basic know-how number 2*,
      pages 160-161)

cake
470g packet buttercake mix
½ quantity fluffy mock cream frosting
   (page 180)
white and black food colouring

decorations
white and black decorating gel

1 Preheat oven to 180°C/160°C fan-forced. Line patty pans with the paper cases.

2 Make cake according to directions on packet. Drop 2 level tablespoons of the mixture into each paper case; bake about 20 minutes. Stand cakes in pans 5 minutes; turn, top-side up, onto wire rack to cool.

3 Divide fluffy mock cream frosting evenly between two small bowls. Tint one bowl white; tint the remaining bowl black. Spread tops of 12 cakes with white frosting; spread remaining cakes with black frosting.

4 Using picture as a guide, pipe clefs and notes onto cakes using white and black gels. Position cakes on prepared board; secure with a little frosting.

equipment

3 x 12-hole (¹⁄₃-cup/80ml) standard
   muffin pans
36 standard paper cases
   (18 yellow, 18 red)
45cm-square prepared cake board
   (see *basic know-how number 2*,
   pages 160-161)

cake

2 x 470g packets buttercake mix
2 quantities butter cream (page 180)
white, red and yellow food colouring

decorations

1 Killer Python
3 snakes (2 blue, 1 green)
4 x 25g Curly Wurly bars
4 Smarties

1 Preheat oven to 180°C/160°C
fan-forced; line muffin pans with
the paper cases.

2 Make cake according to directions
on packets. Drop 2½ level tablespoons
of the mixture into each paper case;
bake about 20 minutes. Stand cakes in
pans 5 minutes; turn, top-side up, onto
wire rack to cool.

3 Place a quarter of the butter cream
into a small bowl; tint white. Divide
remaining butter cream between two
small bowls; tint one bowl red and
the other yellow.

4 Spread red butter cream over tops
of 18 cakes in yellow cases; spread
yellow butter cream over tops of
remaining cakes in red cases.

5 Using picture as a guide, position
cakes on board; secure with a little
butter cream. Place white butter cream
in a piping bag (see *basic know-how
numbers 19-21*, pages 164-165); pipe
numbers one to 36 on cakes.

6 Decorate cakes with Killer Python,
and snakes; use Curly Wurlys for
ladders and Smarties for counters.

snakes&ladders

Piping takes a little skill; practice on a flat surface
before you pipe the numbers on the cakes. You
can buy decorating gel for piping, but we found
that the butter cream was easier to use.

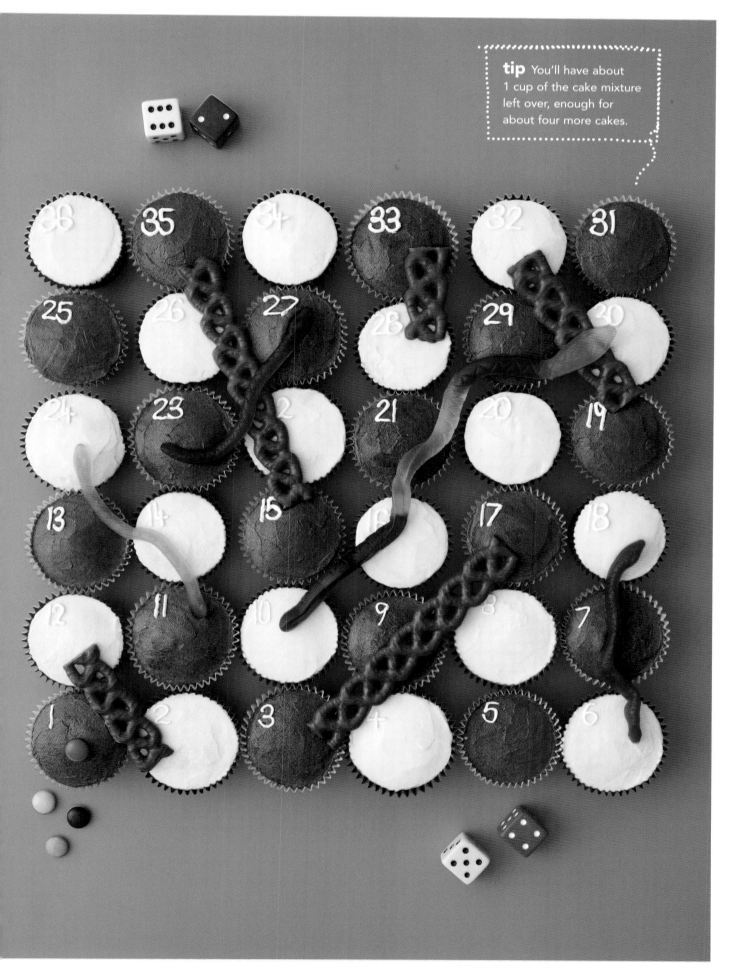

equipment

12-hole (⅓-cup/80ml) standard
    muffin pan
2 x 12-hole (1-tablespoon/20ml)
    mini muffin pans
5 standard paper cases (1 yellow,
    1 green, 1 orange, 1 blue, 1 red)
15 mini muffin paper cases (1 yellow,
    2 green, 3 orange, 4 blue, 5 red)
30cm x 45cm prepared cake board
    (see *basic know-how number 2,*
        pages 160-161)

cake

470g packet buttercake mix
½ quantity butter cream (page 180)
yellow, green, orange, blue and
    red food colouring

decorations

blue, yellow, green and red
    decorating gel
2 blue rainbow choc-chips
3cm red licorice bootlace
14cm black licorice strap,
    cut into strips
2 green sour worms
2 yellow rainbow choc-chips
1 pink musk stick
3 purple triangular jubes
hundreds and thousands
2 rainbow sour worms
2 x 35g tubes mini M&M's

1 Preheat oven to 180°C/160°C
fan-forced. Line standard muffin pan
with the paper cases; line mini muffin
pans with the paper cases.

2 Make cake according to directions
on packet. Drop 2½ level tablespoons
of the mixture into each standard paper
case; bake about 20 minutes. Drop
2 level teaspoons of the mixture into
each mini paper case; bake about
15 minutes. Stand cakes in pans
5 minutes; turn, top-side up, onto wire
rack to cool.

3 Divide butter cream evenly into
five small bowls; tint each bowl with
one of the suggested colours: yellow,
green, orange, blue and red.

4 Using picture as a guide, spread
the cakes with the different coloured
butter creams, matching butter creams
to paper cases. Use different coloured
decorating gels to write the numbers
on the large cakes. Position the large
cakes on the prepared board; secure
with a little butter cream.

5 Using picture as a guide, decorate
the small cakes then position them on
the board next to the appropriate large
cake; secure with a little butter cream.
Spider: Use blue rainbow choc-chips
for eyes, a 1cm strip of red bootlace
for the mouth, and 2cm strips of licorice
strap for the legs.
Snails: Cut 2 x 10cm strips from the
licorice strap; coil each strip onto
cakes to make snails' shells. Cut the
sour worms in half; secure to cakes with
a little butter cream to make snails'
bodies. Using a little butter cream,
secure the yellow choc-chips to top
of the snails' bodies for eyes.

Butterflies: Use strips of musk stick
to make bodies and antennae of the
butterflies; position on cakes. Cut
the jubes in half; dip the cut sides in
hundreds and thousands, position
for wings.
Caterpillar: Cut the sour worms in half;
position three halves along top of cakes
to make the caterpillar's segments.
Use a yellow mini M&M for the eye,
a 2cm strip of red bootlace for the
mouth, and two small strips of licorice
strap for the antennae.
Ladybirds: Cut the licorice strap into
five 3cm strips; position on cakes. Use
yellow mini M&M's for spots and brown
mini M&M's for ladybirds' heads.

tip You'll have about
1½ cups of the cake
mixture left over to make
more cakes for your party.

checkerboard

The hardest part of making this cake is getting the colours right. Use good quality colourings (see *baking info, page 178*) and you'll have no trouble.

equipment
2 x 12-hole (1-tablespoon/20ml) mini muffin pans
24 mini muffin paper cases (12 red, 12 black)
deep 23cm-square cake pan
33cm-square prepared cake board (see *basic know-how number 2, pages 160-161*)

cake
1½ x 470g packets buttercake mix
1 quantity butter cream (page 180)
black and red food colouring

decorations
2 black licorice straps

1 Preheat oven to 180°C/160°C fan-forced. Line mini muffin pans with the paper cases. Grease square cake pan; line base and sides with baking paper, extending paper 5cm over sides (see *basic know-how number 7*, page 160).

2 Make cakes according to directions on packets. Drop 2 level teaspoons of the mixture into each mini paper case; bake about 15 minutes. Stand cakes in pans 5 minutes; turn, top-side up, onto wire rack to cool.

3 Spread remaining cake mixture into square cake pan; bake about 1 hour. Stand cake in pan 5 minutes; turn, top-side up, onto wire rack to cool.

4 Level top of square cake; trim sides to a square shape. Position cake, cut-side down, on prepared board; secure with a little butter cream.

5 Place a quarter of the butter cream in a small bowl; tint black. Tint remaining butter cream red. Spread red butter cream over top and sides of square cake, and over the tops of 12 small cakes in red paper cases.

6 Spread black butter cream over tops of remaining small cakes.

7 Cut licorice straps into 32 squares. Using picture as a guide, press licorice squares gently onto butter cream to make a checkerboard. Cut four strips of licorice long enough to outline the cake. Position some of the cakes on the checkerboard.

hopscotch

Piping takes a little practice. You might find it easier to do the piping, numbering and lettering before using a spatula to position the cakes on the board.

equipment
20cm x 30cm lamington pan
20cm x 50cm prepared cake board
   (see *basic know-how number 2*,
   pages 160-161)

cake
470g packet buttercake mix
2½ quantities butter cream (page 180)
blue, green, yellow and pink
   food colouring

decorations
165g packet mini musks

1 Preheat oven to 180°C/160°C fan-forced. Grease lamington pan; line base and long sides with baking paper, extending paper 5cm over sides.

2 Make cake according to directions on packet. Spread mixture into pan; bake about 35 minutes. Stand cake in pan 5 minutes; turn, top-side up, onto wire rack to cool.

3 Place a fifth of the butter cream into a small bowl; leave plain. Place a third of the remaining butter cream into a small bowl; tint blue. Divide remaining butter cream equally into three small bowls; tint each bowl with one of the remaining colours: green, yellow and pink.

4 Level cake top; turn cake cut-side down. Trim cake to 14cm x 28cm (see *step-by-step number 28*, page 172). Using paper pattern, from pattern sheet provided, cut "home" from cake (see *step-by-step number 29*, pages 172-173). Cut remaining cake into eight 7cm squares.

5 Using picture as a guide, spread some of the green butter cream over tops and sides of two hopscotch squares; repeat with yellow, pink and blue butter cream. Spread remaining blue butter cream over top and sides of "home" cake. Position cakes on prepared board; secure with a little butter cream.

6 Place plain butter cream in piping bag (see *basic know-how numbers 19-21*, pages 164-165). Pipe around edges of each hopscotch square and "home" cake. Using picture as a guide, use mini musks to make "home" and the numbers one to eight.

tip You'll have about 1½ cups of the cake mixture left over; make more noughts and crosses cakes for your guests.

noughts&crosses

This is a very easy birthday cake to make; it is suitable for boys and girls alike. You can make it in any colour you like.

equipment
12-hole (⅓-cup/80ml) standard muffin pan
10 standard paper cases (5 red, 5 white)
30cm-square prepared cake board (see *basic know-how number 2*, pages 160-161)

cake
470g packet buttercake mix
½ quantity butter cream (page 180)
red and white food colouring

decorations
8 musk sticks
5 red fruit rings
18g packet white Tic Tacs

1 Preheat oven to 180°C/160°C fan-forced. Line muffin pan with the paper cases.

2 Make cake according to directions on packet. Drop 2½ tablespoons of the mixture into each paper case; bake about 20 minutes. Stand cakes in pan 5 minutes; turn, top-side up, onto wire rack to cool.

3 Divide butter cream equally into two small bowls; tint one bowl red and the other white.

4 Spread red butter cream over five cakes in red cases, and white butter cream over the remaining five cakes in the white cases.

5 Use musk sticks to make noughts and crosses grid; secure to prepared board with a little butter cream. Using picture as a guide, position cakes on board; secure with a little butter cream. Top white cakes with fruit rings for noughts; use Tic Tacs to make crosses on the red cakes.

4

5

numbers

6

one

equipment

12-hole (⅓-cup/80ml) standard
    muffin pan
6 standard paper cases (blue)
3.5cm- and 6.5cm-wide
    duck-shaped cutters
new clean small paint brush
20cm x 50cm prepared cake board
    (see *basic know-how number 2,*
        pages 160-161)

cake

½ x 470g packet buttercake mix
½ quantity butter cream (page 180)
blue food colouring

decorations

¼ cup (40g) icing sugar
100g ready-made white icing
    (page 180)
yellow and orange food colouring
6 blue rainbow choc-chips

1 Preheat oven to 180°C/160°C
fan-forced. Line muffin pan with
the paper cases.

2 Make cake according to directions
on packet. Drop 2½ level tablespoons
of the mixture into each paper case;
bake about 20 minutes. Stand cakes in
pan 5 minutes; turn, top-side up, onto
wire rack to cool.

3 On a surface dusted with sifted
icing sugar, knead the ready-made
icing until smooth; tint with yellow
colouring (see *basic know-how number
16*, page 162). Roll icing until 3mm
thick; using cutters, cut two large
ducks and five small ducks from the
icing. Brush one side of a large duck
sparingly, but evenly, with water.
Gently press the other large duck
onto the wet surface.

4 Using the paint brush, paint an
orange beak on each side of the
mother duck's head. Gently press blue
rainbow choc-chips into the icing to
make the eyes. Lay mother duck flat on
a baking-paper-lined tray to dry. Paint
beaks and position eyes on ducklings;
dry on tray with mother duck.

5 Tint butter cream blue; spread
over tops of cakes. Position cakes
on prepared board to resemble the
number 1; secure with a little butter
cream. Using picture as a guide, position
mother duck and ducklings on cakes.

equipment

12-hole (⅓-cup/80ml) standard
    muffin pan
12 standard paper cases
    (6 green, 6 brown)
30cm x 45cm prepared cake board
    (see *basic know-how number 2*,
    pages 160-161)

cake

470g packet buttercake mix
½ quantity butter cream (page 180)
green food colouring
3 teaspoons cocoa powder

decorations

black and red decorating gel
6 banana lollies
6 brown rainbow choc-chips
1 x 30cm (3mm) brown chenille stick
    (pipe cleaner)
edible silver glitter
3 sour worms
35g tube mini M&M's
7 mint leaves

1 Preheat oven to 180°C/160°C fan-forced. Line muffin pan with the paper cases.

2 Make cake according to directions on packet. Drop 2½ level tablespoons of the mixture into each paper case; bake about 20 minutes. Stand cakes in pan 5 minutes; turn, top-side up, onto wire rack to cool.

3 Tint half the butter cream green. Divide remaining butter cream into two small bowls. Stir 2 teaspoons of the sifted cocoa into one bowl; stir remaining sifted cocoa into remaining butter cream.

4 Using the cakes in the brown paper cases, spread the dark brown butter cream over three cakes; spread the light brown butter cream over three cakes.

5 Using picture as a guide, use the black decorating gel to draw spirals on the brown cakes for snails' shells. Position bananas for bodies. Use the red decorating gel to pipe mouths on the snails. Secure the rainbow choc-chips for eyes with a little butter cream. Cut the chenille stick into 12 x 2.5cm pieces; position in cakes for feelers.

6 Using picture as a guide, spread green butter cream over remaining cakes. Sprinkle glitter carefully over each cake to make snails' trails. Using the handle of a teaspoon, make a small hole in three of the cakes; gently push worms into position (see *step-by-step number 32*, pages 172-173). Decorate cakes with mini M&M's and mint leaves.

7 Assemble cakes on prepared board in the shape of the number 2. Secure with a little butter cream.

We set this cake up on artificial grass instead of a board. To create a wonderful world for an insect-themed party, cover the party table with the grass and decorate the table with different types of plastic insects.

tips You'll have 1 cup of the cake mixture left over; use it to make more cakes for your guests.
We used the mouse traps as a prop in the photo; it's best not to use them at a children's party because of safety concerns.

equipment

12-hole (⅓-cup/80ml) standard
   muffin pan
11 standard paper cases
1.5cm-round cutter
35cm x 45cm prepared cake board
   (see *basic know-how number 2*,
   pages 160-161)

cake

470g packet buttercake mix
1 quantity butter cream (page 180)
yellow and pink food colouring

decorations

¼ cup (40g) icing sugar
60g ready-made white icing
   (page 180)
2 large pink marshmallows, halved
5 large white marshmallows, halved
35g tube mini M&M's
3 pink Mallow Bakes, halved
1 white Mallow Bake, halved
1m length black licorice bootlace

th**ree**

Three year olds love nursery rhymes, and even though the mice are clearly not blind – they're having fun finding the cheese.

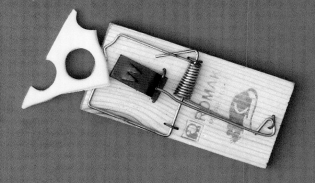

1 Preheat oven to 180°C/160°C fan-forced. Line muffin pan with the paper cases.

2 Make cake according to directions on packet. Drop 2½ level tablespoons of the mixture into each paper case; bake about 20 minutes. Stand cakes in pan 5 minutes; turn, top-side up, onto wire rack to cool.

3 Divide butter cream into four small bowls. Tint one bowl yellow, tint remaining bowls various shades of pink (light, medium, dark).

4 Spread yellow butter cream over four cakes. Using picture as a guide, spread pink butter cream over remaining seven cakes.

5 On a surface dusted with sifted icing sugar, knead the ready-made icing until smooth; tint yellow (see *basic know-how number 16*, page 162). Roll icing until 3mm thick. Cut out 2 x 5cm squares. Cut a few 1.5cm rounds from the squares to give the look of swiss cheese; cut each square into two triangles. Position cheese triangles on yellow cakes.

6 Using picture as a guide, position marshmallow halves for ears and mini M&M's for eyes. Position Mallow Bake halves for noses. Cut 28 x 1cm pieces from licorice bootlace; use these to make whiskers. Position cakes on prepared board to resemble the number 3; secure with a little butter cream. Cut 7 x 10cm pieces from licorice bootlace to make tails; push into cakes.

fur

A cupcake on a cupcake is going to delight girls of any age. They're not difficult to make, but it will take a little time to make the cupcake shapes.

equipment

12-hole (⅓-cup/80ml) standard
    muffin pan
9 standard paper cases (blue)
4.5cm-round cutter
fluted pastry wheel
30cm x 45cm prepared cake board
    (see *basic know-how number 2*,
    pages 160-161)

cake

470g packet buttercake mix
½ quantity butter cream (page 180)
blue, pink and yellow food colouring

decorations

½ cup (80g) icing sugar
200g ready-made white icing
    (page 180)
yellow, green and pink food colouring
2 red mini M&M's
hundreds and thousands
60g jar mixed cachous

1 Preheat oven to 180°C/160°C fan-forced. Line muffin pan with the paper cases.

2 Make cake according to directions on packet. Drop 2½ level tablespoons of the mixture into each paper case; bake about 20 minutes. Stand cakes in pan 5 minutes; turn, top-side up, onto wire rack to cool.

3 Divide butter cream equally into three small bowls; tint each bowl with one of the suggested colours: blue, pink and yellow. Spread blue butter cream over three cakes, pink butter cream over two cakes and yellow butter cream over four cakes.

4 On a surface dusted with sifted icing sugar, knead the ready-made icing until smooth. Divide icing into three equal portions; tint each portion with one of the suggested colours: yellow, green and pink (see *basic know-how number 16*, page 162). Roll each portion until 3mm thick.

5 Cut two 4.5cm rounds from the yellow icing; cut three 4.5cm rounds from the green icing; cut four 4.5cm rounds from the pink icing. Cut each round in half for the cupcake "tops". Using picture as a guide, position "tops" on cakes.

6 Working with one icing portion at a time, use a fluted pastry wheel to cut a 3cm x 18cm strip from yellow, green and pink icings. Cut two yellow, three pink and four green patty case "bases" from each strip of icing (see *step-by-step number 30*, page 173). Mark vertical lines on each of the "bases" (see *step-by-step number 31*, page 172). Position "bases" on cakes.

7 Brush a tiny amount of water onto tops of the cupcake "tops" and "bases"; decorate with mini M&M's, hundreds and thousands and cachous.

8 Position cakes on prepared board to resemble the number 4; secure with a little butter cream.

five

equipment

12-hole (⅓-cup/80ml) standard
  muffin pan
11 standard paper cases (orange)
35cm x 45cm prepared cake board
  (see *basic know-how number 2*,
    pages 160-161)

cake

470g packet buttercake mix
½ quantity butter cream (page 180)
orange and pink food colouring

decorations

4 x 35g tubes mini M&M's
3 small pink jelly beans,
  halved crossways
1 musk stick, cut into thin strips
1 red sour strap, cut into
  10 x 2cm strips
10 large pink candy hearts

1 Preheat oven to 180°C/160°C fan-forced. Line muffin pan with the paper cases.

2 Make cake according to directions on packet. Drop 2½ level tablespoons of the mixture into each paper case; bake about 20 minutes. Stand cakes in pan 5 minutes; turn, top-side up, onto wire rack to cool.

3 Divide butter cream into two small bowls; tint one bowl of butter cream orange, tint the other bowl pink. Spread orange butter cream over the tops of five cakes; spread pink butter cream over the remaining six cakes.

4 Using picture as a guide, assemble cakes on the prepared board in the shape of the number 5; secure with a little butter cream. Decorate each pink cake using orange mini M&M's to make heart shapes.

5 Decorate the five remaining kitty face cakes using the pink mini M&M's for eyes and jelly bean halves for the noses. Cut the musk stick strips into 20 x 2.5cm lengths; use for whiskers. Shape and position two lengths of the sour strap strips for mouths. Use the hearts to make the ears for each kitty.

equipment

12-hole (⅓-cup/80ml) standard
  muffin pan
12 standard paper cases
  (5 green, 4 brown, 3 blue)
40cm x 50cm prepared cake board
  (see *basic know-how number 2,*
  pages 160-161)

cake

470g packet buttercake mix
1 quantity butter cream (page 180)
green and blue food colouring
1 tablespoon cocoa powder

decorations

2 plain chocolate biscuits, crushed
25g Curly Wurly bar
5 green snakes, heads removed
11 mint leaves, halved lengthways
9 ready-made icing flowers
4 jelly-filled strawberries
2 sour worms
5 licorice allsorts
2 ready-made icing butterflies
2 foil-wrapped chocolate ladybirds

1 Preheat oven to 180°C/160°C
fan-forced. Line muffin pan with
the paper cases.

2 Make cake according to directions
on packet. Drop 2½ level tablespoons
of the mixture into each paper case;
bake about 20 minutes. Stand cakes in
pan 5 minutes; turn, top-side up, onto
wire rack to cool.

3 Tint half the butter cream green.
Divide remaining butter cream between
two small bowls; tint one bowl blue.
Stir the sifted cocoa into the remaining
butter cream.

4 Spread each butter cream over the
tops of cakes, matching the colour of
the paper cases with the colour of the
butter cream. Sprinkle brown-coloured
cakes with crushed chocolate biscuits.

5 Using picture as a guide, assemble
cakes on prepared board to resemble
the number 6; secure with a little
butter cream. Use the Curly Wurly to
make a trellis; intertwine the snakes to
resemble vines. Decorate with mint
leaves and icing flowers.

6 Decorate brown cakes with jelly-
filled strawberries and mint leaves.
Using the end of a teaspoon, make a
small hole in two of the brown cakes;
gently push one end of the sour
worms into the holes (see *step-by-step
number 32,* pages 172-173).

7 Cut coloured layers of the licorice
allsorts into the shape of a shovel,
bucket and watering can; position on
blue cakes. Position butterflies and
ladybirds on the cakes.

Many children like gardening, so take-home treats
could be small gardening tools. The artificial grass
we used for the number 2 cake (see page 126) is
ideal to use as a background for this cake.

tip You'll have ¾ cup of the
cake mixture left over, enough
for another three cakes.

tip Use left over cake mixture to make extra cakes for the party.

equipment

12-hole (1/3-cup/80ml) standard
   muffin pan
9 standard paper cases
   (5 blue, 4 green)
30cm x 45cm prepared cake board
   (see *basic know-how number 2*,
   pages 160-161)

cake

470g packet buttercake mix
½ quantity butter cream (page 180)
blue and green food colouring

decorations

2 tablespoons desiccated coconut
7 after-dinner mints
13 scorched peanuts
1 teaspoon red, orange and yellow
   BoPeep lollies, chopped coarsely
1 red jelly baby
1 mint leaf, sliced finely
3 small plastic crocodile toys
1 plastic tree
1 x 30cm (3mm) green chenille stick
   (pipe cleaner)
1 x 30cm piece red licorice bootlace
1 yellow fruit stick

1 Preheat oven to 180°C/160°C fan-forced. Line muffin pan with the paper cases.

2 Make cake according to directions on packet. Drop 2½ level tablespoons of the mixture into each paper case; bake about 20 minutes. Stand cakes in pan 5 minutes; turn, top-side up, onto wire rack to cool.

3 Divide butter cream evenly into two small bowls; tint one bowl blue and the other green. Spread blue butter cream over cakes in blue cases to resemble water; spread green butter cream over remaining cakes to make camping ground. Position cakes on prepared board to make the number 7; secure with a little butter cream.

4 Place coconut and a few drops of green colouring in a small plastic bag; rub until coconut is evenly covered (see *basic know-how number 25*, page 164). Using picture as a guide, sprinkle coconut over cakes to make grass.

5 Working quickly, use a hot metal spatula to melt one edge on two after-dinner mints; pressing gently, join the melted edges together on an angle to make part of the tent (see *step-by-step number 33*, page 173). Repeat with two more after-dinner mints; position tent on cakes.

6 Using picture as a guide, use some of the scorched peanuts and chopped BoPeeps to make a campfire; position jelly baby near the campfire. Position slices of mint leaf for water reeds; position crocodiles and the tree. Use remaining scorched peanuts for rocks. Shape two after-dinner mints into rock platforms; position at the water's edge.

7 To make a flying fox, cut small pieces of chenille stick and use to secure one end of the licorice bootlace to the plastic tree and the other end of the bootlace to a small segment of the fruit stick. Gently push the fruit stick into one of the green cakes. Shape a small piece of chenille stick to make flying fox handle bars; position on the licorice bootlace. Trim the remaining after-dinner mint to make a platform at the end of the flying fox.

seven

Kids love to go camping. If you have a large enough grassed area at home, turn the area into a camping ground for the party. It's an easy, inexpensive party theme.

tip The traffic lights can be made several hours ahead; leave them flat so that the butter cream becomes firm. If the weather or room is hot, put the traffic lights in the fridge, then position them on the cake at party time.

eight

equipment
2 x 12-hole (⅓-cup/80ml) standard muffin pans
16 standard paper cases (yellow)
30cm x 45cm prepared cake board (see *basic know-how number 2*, pages 160-161)

cake
470g packet buttercake mix
1 quantity butter cream (page 180)
blue food colouring
⅓ cup (35g) cocoa powder

decorations
1 x 55g Cherry Ripe bar
2 x 25g Curly Wurly bars
1 roll black licorice strap
1 jelly baby
2 red mini M&M's
2 yellow mini M&M's
2 green mini M&M's
2 ice-block sticks
1 large round green jube
small toy vehicles

1 Preheat oven to 180°C/160°C fan-forced. Line muffin pans with the paper cases.

2 Make cake according to directions on packet. Drop 2½ level tablespoons of the mixture into each paper case; bake about 20 minutes. Stand cakes in pans 5 minutes; turn, top-side up, onto wire rack to cool.

3 Transfer 2 level tablespoons of the butter cream to a small bowl; tint with blue colouring. Stir sifted cocoa into the remaining butter cream.

4 Spread chocolate butter cream over tops of 14 cakes. Remove paper cases from remaining two cakes; trim a third off the bases of the cakes, then spread tops with blue butter cream.

5 Using picture as a guide, assemble cakes on the prepared board in the shape of the number 8; secure with a little butter cream.

6 Using the blade of a hot metal spatula, melt long edges of the Cherry Ripe (see *step-by-step number 33*, page 173); attach the two Curly Wurly bars on either side of the Cherry Ripe to make a bridge. Stand a few minutes to set, then position over the blue cakes.

7 Cut licorice strap into thin strips (see *basic know-how number 24*, page 165); using picture as a guide, use strips to make road markings. Cut licorice into thicker strips to make a pedestrian crossing; position the jelly baby as a pedestrian; secure with a little butter cream.

8 Cut two pieces of licorice to hold the traffic lights. Use a tiny amount of butter cream to attach the M&M's to the licorice; lay flat until firm. Attach the licorice pieces to the ice-block sticks with a little more butter cream; lay flat until firm before positioning upright in the cakes.

9 Use the jube for a roundabout. Position the vehicles.

nine

Scrapbooking has opened up a whole new world for us. These dreamy little cakes look wonderful with the tiny flowers, available from craft stores, encircling each candle. We used about 9 flowers on each candle, each packet contains 18 flowers. To position the candles firmly on the cakes, cut and remove the centre from the rounds of icing.

equipment
12-hole (⅓-cup/80ml) standard
    muffin pan
11 standard paper cases (purple)
7cm-round fluted cutter
3.5cm-round cutter
40cm x 50cm prepared cake board
    (see *basic know-how number 2*,
      pages 160-161)

cake
470g packet buttercake mix
⅓ cup (110g) apricot jam,
    warmed, strained
½ cup (80g) icing sugar
250g ready-made white icing
    (page 180)
pink and mauve food colouring

decorations
5 packets purple scrapbooking flowers
2 packets pink scrapbooking flowers
11 tea-light candles

1 Preheat oven to 180°C/160°C fan-forced. Line muffin pan with the paper cases.

2 Make cake according to directions on packet. Drop 2½ level tablespoons of the mixture into each paper case; bake about 20 minutes. Stand cakes in pan 5 minutes; turn, top-side up, onto wire rack to cool.

3 Lightly brush tops of cake with jam. On a surface dusted with sifted icing sugar, knead the ready-made icing until smooth; divide icing into three equal portions. Tint one portion pink and one portion mauve (see *basic know-how number 16*, page 162); leave the remaining portion white. Roll out each colour, one at a time, until 3mm thick.

4 Cut three 7cm fluted rounds from the pink icing, cut four rounds from the mauve icing and cut four rounds from the white icing; position on tops of cakes. Cut 3.5cm rounds from the centre of each icing round; discard centre cut-outs.

5 Attach scrapbooking flowers around the side of each candle; position candle in the centre of each cake.

6 Using picture as a guide, position cakes on prepared board in the shape of the number 9; secure with a little butter cream.

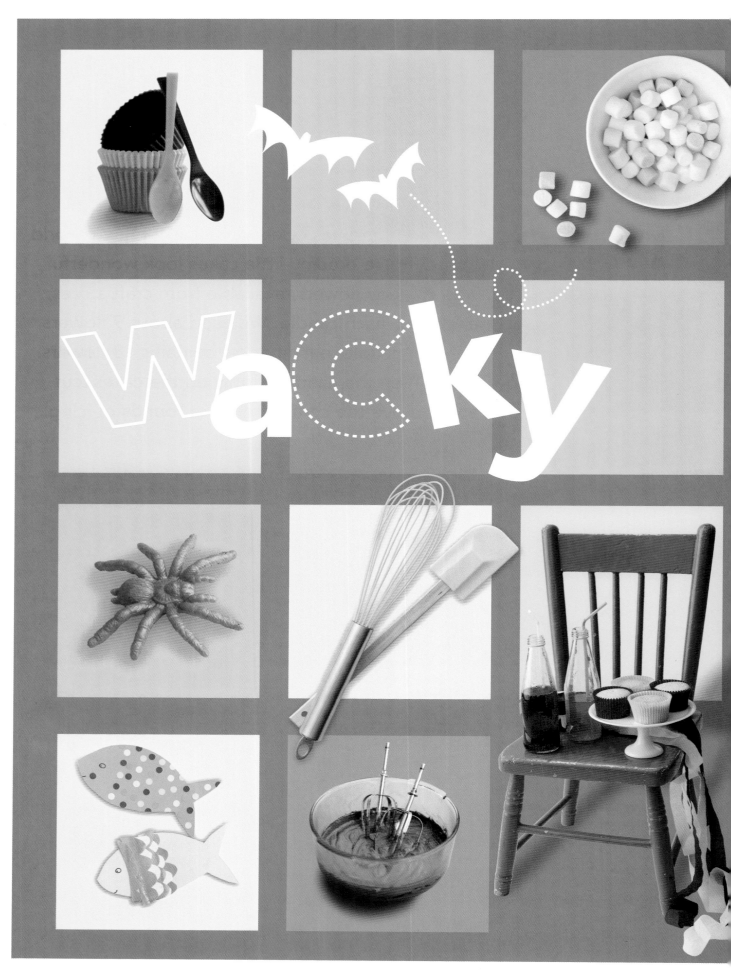

Wacky

solar system

equipment

deep 30cm-round cake pan
2 x 20cm x 30cm lamington pans
2 bamboo skewers
3cm, 4cm, 6cm and 9cm-round cutters
40cm x 1m prepared cake board
    (see *basic know-how number 2*,
    pages 160-161)

cake

4 x 470g packets buttercake mix
3 quantities butter cream (page 180)
orange, red, yellow, blue, green,
    and black food colouring

decorations

3 rainbow sour straps, cut
    yellow strips from strap

1 Preheat oven to 180°C/160°C fan-forced. Grease and line round cake pan (see *basic know-how numbers 3-6*, pages 160-161). Grease lamington pans; line base and long sides with baking paper, extending paper 5cm over sides.

2 Make two cakes according to directions on packets, spread into round pan; bake about 50 minutes. Stand cake in pan 10 minutes; turn top-side up onto wire rack to cool.

3 Make remaining cakes according to directions on packets. Divide mixture between lamington pans; bake about 35 minutes. Stand cakes in pans 5 minutes; turn, top-side up, onto wire rack to cool.

4 Level lamington cake tops; turn cut-side down. Use round cake to make the Sun and lamington cakes to make the planets. Cut two 3cm-rounds to make Mercury and Pluto.

Cut three 4cm-rounds to make Venus, Mars and Earth. Cut two 6cm-rounds to make Uranus and Neptune. Cut a 9cm-round from cake to make Jupiter. Using paper pattern, from pattern sheet provided, cut out Saturn.

5 Place two-thirds of the butter cream in a medium bowl; tint dark orange. Place half the remaining butter cream in a small bowl; tint medium orange. Divide remaining butter cream equally into four small bowls; leave one bowl plain and tint each remaining bowl with one of the suggested colours: red, blue and green.

6 Position the round cake, top-side up, at the end of the prepared board; secure with a little butter cream. Starting from the Sun, and working left to right, position and secure (with a little butter cream) each planet to the prepared board as you finish it.

1 sun

Using picture as a guide, spread about two-thirds of the dark orange butter cream over the top and side of the Sun; roughen with a fork. Dip a bamboo skewer into red colouring, pull through the butter cream to resemble flares.

2 mercury

Spread top and side of a 3cm cake with dark orange butter cream; roughen with a fork. Dip a bamboo skewer into yellow colouring and pull through the butter cream.

3 venus

Spread top and side of a 4cm cake with medium orange butter cream blended with a little dark orange butter cream.

4 earth

Spread top and side of a 4cm cake with blue butter cream; dot with a little green butter cream to resemble land on Earth's surface.

5 mars

Spread top and side of a 4cm cake with red butter cream blended with a little dark orange butter cream.

6 jupiter

Spread top and side of a 9cm cake with red butter cream blended with a little dark orange butter cream and plain butter cream to create bands of colour across the planet.

7 saturn

Tint 1 tablespoon of the plain butter cream yellow. Spread top and side of Saturn and Saturn's rings with medium orange butter cream blended with a little yellow and dark orange butter cream. Top Saturn's rings with yellow strips from sour straps.

8 uranus

Spread top and side of a 6cm cake with blended blue and green butter cream.

9 neptune

Spread top and side of a 6cm cake with blue butter cream.

10 pluto

Tint 1 tablespoon of the plain butter cream with black food colouring to make grey. Spread top and side of a 3cm cake with grey butter cream; blend a little blue butter cream over the top of the grey and swirl through the butter cream.

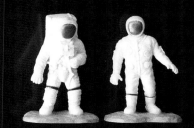

Most children love lamingtons. We've used a lot of them to make this spectacular pyramid – just watch it be devoured. Don't forget a desert-sand coloured background. For an Egyptian-themed party have the guests come in fancy dress.

pharaoh's pyramid

equipment
50cm-square prepared cake board
(see *basic know-how number 2*,
pages 160-161)

cake
7 x 350g packets lamington fingers
(18 in each packet)

decorations
plastic Egyptian-themed toys

1 Assemble lamingtons on prepared board to make a 30cm-square base; trim lamingtons to fit.

2 Using picture as a guide, build up pyramid with remaining lamingtons eight layers high; trim lamingtons as required to fit pyramid shape.

3 Decorate pyramid with toys.

tip You could use chenille sticks (pipe cleaners) for arms instead of the twigs.

snow folk

We used cotton wool to create a snowy effect. Use your imagination when you're "dressing" the snow folk and use whatever "clothes" you like.

equipment
6-hole (¾-cup/180ml) texas muffin pan
12-hole (⅓-cup/80ml) standard
   muffin pan
40cm-square prepared cake board
   (see *basic know-how number 2*,
      pages 160-161)
2.5cm-round cutter

cake
½ x 470g packet buttercake mix
1 quantity fluffy frosting (page 180)

decorations
3 giant white marshmallows
2 teaspoons icing sugar
10g ready-made white icing
   (page 180)
orange food colouring
1 red licorice strap
1 black licorice strap
3 pink mini M&M's
100g packet Mallow Bakes, halved
6 small cleaned sticks or twigs
1 pink cocktail umbrella
1 black licorice rope

1 Preheat oven to 180°C/160°C fan-forced. Grease three holes of the texas muffin pan; grease three holes of the standard muffin pan.

2 Make cake according to directions on packet. Drop ⅓ cup of the mixture into greased texas pan holes; bake about 25 minutes. Drop 2½ level tablespoons of the mixture into the greased standard pan holes; bake about 20 minutes. Stand cakes in pans 5 minutes; turn, top-side up, onto wire rack to cool.

3 Level cake tops; trim cakes into rounded shapes (see *step-by-step number 3*, page 167). Turn larger cakes upside down. Place smaller cakes, top-side up, on top of larger cakes; secure with a little fluffy frosting. Spread cakes all over with frosting. Place marshmallows on top of small cakes for heads. Position cakes on prepared board.

4 On a surface dusted with sifted icing sugar, knead the ready-made icing until smooth. Tint with orange colouring (see *basic know-how number 16*, page 162). Mould into three carrot shapes for noses.

5 Make snowgirl using picture as a guide. Cut a bow from the red licorice strap and eyes from the black licorice strap. Secure bow, eyes and nose to head with a little frosting. Use pink M&M's for buttons. Position Mallow Bakes around bottom of snowgirl for skirt. Position twigs for arms, and the umbrella on the snowgirl.

6 Make snowmen using picture as a guide. Cut buttons, bow and scarf from black licorice strap; position on bodies. Cut eyes from black licorice strap. Secure eyes and noses with a little frosting. Position twigs for arms. Make hats by cutting two 1.5cm rounds from the licorice strap; secure to the heads with a little frosting. Cut two 1cm pieces from the licorice rope; secure to the base of the hats with a little frosting.

1

2

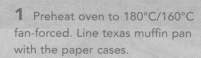

equipment
6-hole (¾-cup/180ml) texas muffin pan
5 texas muffin paper cases

cake
½ x 470g packet buttercake mix
½ x quantity butter cream (page 180)
yellow, blue, green, purple and
   brown food colouring

decorations
purple funny face
2 pink Allen's doughnuts
2 small yellow jelly beans
1 Jaffa
1 freckle, halved
1 red sour strap

green funny face
2 brown mini M&M's
1 Jaffa
7cm piece black licorice strap
1 candy orange wedge

brown funny face
7cm piece black licorice strap
1 strawberry and cream lolly, halved
1 red jelly bean
1 sour worm

blue funny face
2 blue mini M&M's
2 round peppermints
1 small yellow jelly bean
6cm piece black licorice strap
1 yellow fruit stick

yellow funny face
2 blue mini M&M's
2 round peppermints
1 small orange jelly bean
3cm piece red licorice strap
2 candy orange wedges

1 Preheat oven to 180°C/160°C
fan-forced. Line texas muffin pan
with the paper cases.

2 Make cake according to directions
on packet. Drop ⅓ cup of mixture into
each paper case; bake about 25 minutes.
Stand cakes in pan 5 minutes; turn,
top-side up, onto wire rack to cool.

3 Divide butter cream equally into
five small bowls; tint each bowl with
one of the suggested colours: yellow,
blue, green, purple and brown.

5

funny faces

1 purple funny face
Spread purple butter cream over top of one cake. Using picture as a guide, position doughnut lollies for eyes and jelly beans for eyebrows. Position Jaffa for nose and freckle halves for ears. Shape and trim red sour strap to make mouth.

2 green funny face
Spread green butter cream over top of one cake. Using picture as a guide, position M&M's for eyes and Jaffa for nose. Shape and trim a strip of licorice to make mouth and hat brim; top with candy orange wedge to make hat.

3 brown funny face
Spread brown butter cream over top of one cake. Using picture as a guide, trim and position licorice strap. Secure strawberry and cream halves to licorice strap with a little butter cream for eyes. Position jelly bean for nose and sour worm for mouth.

4 blue funny face
Spread blue butter cream over top of one cake. Secure mini M&M's to peppermints with a little butter cream; position for eyes. Using picture as a guide, position jelly bean for nose. Shape a strip of the licorice to make mouth; position on cake. Cut yellow fruit stick into thin strips; position on cake for hair.

5 yellow funny face
Spread yellow butter cream over top of one cake. Secure mini M&M's to peppermints with a little butter cream; position for eyes. Using picture as a guide, position jelly bean for nose. Shape licorice into tongue; position on cake. Position candy orange wedges for ears.

tip You'll have enough cake mixture left over to make one more funny face.

crazy clowns

A row of clown faces on a party table decorated with streamers and party whistles would look great. Pushing the "hair" into the cakes is a bit fiddly, and needs to be done about an hour before the party.

equipment
12-hole (1/3-cup/80ml) standard
   muffin pan
4 standard paper cases
   (1 pink, 1 purple, 1 green, 1 yellow)
4cm-round cutter
bamboo skewer

cake
470g packet buttercake mix
1 quantity butter cream (page 180)
white, yellow, pink, purple and
   green food colouring

decorations
hundreds and thousands
8 green mini musks
4 x red mini M&M's
1 red licorice rope,
   cut into 4 x 5cm pieces
120cm blue sugar-coated bootlace,
   cut into 24 x 5cm lengths
120cm red sugar-coated bootlace,
   cut into 24 x 5cm lengths
200g packet small jelly beans

1 Preheat oven to 180°C/160°C fan-forced. Line the muffin pan with four paper cases; grease another four holes of the muffin pan.

2 Make cake according to directions on packet. Drop 2½ level tablespoons of the mixture into each of the eight prepared holes; bake about 20 minutes. Stand cakes in pan 5 minutes; turn, top-side up, onto wire rack to cool.

3 Transfer half the butter cream into a small bowl; tint white. Divide remaining butter cream into four small bowls; tint each bowl with one of the suggested colours: yellow, pink, purple and green.

4 Using the four cakes in paper cases, mark a circle with the 4cm-round cutter on the top of each cake. Using a small pointed knife, cut around the circle and down about 2cm into the cakes, holding the knife at an angle to make cone-shaped hats for the clowns (see *step-by-step 34*, page 172).

5 Spread top edge of each cake still in its paper case with one of the coloured butter creams (do not spread butter cream into the hole).

6 Using the four cakes without paper cases, and using a small serrated knife, trim the cakes into round shapes for the clowns' heads (see *step-by-step number 35*, pages 172-173). Spread the heads with the white butter cream. Using picture as a guide, position heads on top of the cakes in paper cases.

7 Spread top of the clowns' hats with white butter cream; roll in hundreds and thousands. Position hats on clowns' heads. Using picture as a guide, position mini musks for eyes and mini M&M's for nose. Shape licorice rope into mouth.

8 Use skewer to make six small holes in both sides of clowns' heads; push a length of sugar-coated bootlace into each hole (see *step-by-step number 36*, page 173).

9 Position jelly beans around each head to make clowns' frills.

tip You will have enough cake mixture left over to make about another five clowns – you'll need more butter cream and lollies to decorate them, though.

kaleidoscopes

Make as many kaleidoscopes as you have guests, then arrange them on a large round platter or board, like a wheel, they will look fantastic. These cakes are not difficult to make, just a bit fiddly.

equipment
6-hole (¾-cup/180ml) texas muffin pan
6 texas muffin paper cases
   (2 green, 2 red, 2 yellow)

cake
470g packet buttercake mix
½ quantity butter cream (page 180)
green, purple and yellow
   food colouring

decorations
kaleidoscope one
2 triangular orange jubes
1 square orange jube
1 orange Life Saver
8 yellow mini musks
5 green mini musks

kaleidoscope two
2 green Life Savers
1 orange Life Saver
8 orange mini M&M's
12 green mini M&M's

kaleidoscope three
1 pink "Double D" sugar-free drop
3 pink Life Savers
6 green mini musks
19 yellow mini musks

kaleidoscope four
1 round orange jube
1 square red jube
5 yellow mini M&M's
16 pink mini musks

kaleidoscope five
3 yellow Life Savers
9 yellow mini M&M's
18 red mini M&M's
1 red "Double D" sugar-free drop

kaleidoscope six
1 round green jube
1 square green jube
3 yellow mini M&M's
3 pink "Double D" sugar-free drops
6 pink mini musks

tip You'll have 1 cup of the cake mixture left over, enough to make three more kaleidoscopes.

1 Preheat oven to 180°C/160°C fan-forced. Line texas muffin pan with the paper cases.

2 Make cake according to directions on packet. Drop ⅓ cup of the mixture into each paper case; bake about 25 minutes. Stand cakes in pan 5 minutes; turn, top-side up, onto wire rack to cool.

3 Divide butter cream into three small bowls; tint each bowl with one of the suggested colours: green, purple and yellow.

kaleidoscope one
Spread green butter cream over top of one cake. Cut triangular jubes in half. Cut square jube in half; cut halves into triangles. Using picture as a guide, decorate cake with lollies listed at left.

kaleidoscope two
Spread yellow butter cream over top of one cake. Cut green Life Savers in half. Using picture as a guide, decorate cake with lollies listed at left.

kaleidoscope three
Spread purple butter cream over top of one cake. Using picture as a guide, decorate cake with lollies listed at left.

kaleidoscope four
Spread yellow butter cream over top of one cake. Cut round jube in half, use one half only. Cut square jube in half; cut halves into triangles. Using picture as a guide, decorate cake with lollies listed at left.

kaleidoscope five
Spread purple butter cream over top of one cake. Using picture as a guide, decorate cake with lollies listed at left.

kaleidoscope six
Spread green butter cream over top of one cake. Cut round jube in half, use one half only. Cut square jube in half; cut halves into triangles, use three triangles only. Using picture as a guide, decorate cake with lollies listed at left.

juggling jamie

equipment

8-hole (½-cup/125ml) mini loaf pan
9-hole (½-cup/125ml) friand pan
2 x 12-hole (1-tablespoon/20ml)
    mini muffin pans
1cm star cutter
45cm x 55cm prepared cake board
    (see *basic know-how number 2*,
        pages 160-161)

cake

1½ x 470g packets buttercake mix
1 quantity butter cream (page 180)
blue, purple, green, orange, red
    and pink food colouring

decorations

6 green Smarties
6 blue Smarties
3 fruit allsorts
18 red mini M&M's
2 red fruit rings, halved
100g packet red bootlace
2 blue mini M&M's
2 round peppermints
1 freckle
1 red Smartie
1 green sour strap
10 small pink jelly beans

1 Preheat oven to 170°C/150°C fan-forced. Grease five holes of the mini loaf pan; grease eight holes of the friand pan; grease 15 holes of the mini muffin pans.

2 Make cake according to directions on packets. Drop ⅓ cup of the mixture into greased mini loaf pan holes; drop 2½ level tablespoons of the mixture into greased friand pan holes. Bake cakes about 25 minutes. Stand cakes in pans 5 minutes; turn, top-side up, onto wire rack to cool.

3 Drop 3 level teaspoons of the mixture into greased mini muffin pan holes; bake about 15 minutes. Stand cakes in pans 5 minutes; turn, top-side up, onto wire rack to cool.

4 Divide butter cream into six small bowls; tint each bowl with one of the suggested colours: blue, purple, green, orange, red and pale pink.

5 Using picture as a guide, spread the butter cream over tops of cakes.

6 Using picture as a guide, assemble cakes on prepared board; secure with a little butter cream. Use three mini muffin cakes for each foot and two loaf cakes for each leg. Use one loaf cake and two friand cakes for the body. Use two friand cakes for each arm and one mini muffin cake for each hand.

7 Use two friand cakes for the face, two mini muffin cakes for ears and one mini muffin cake for nose. Use four mini muffin cakes for the juggling balls.

8 Position green and blue Smarties on the legs. Slice two fruit allsorts into quarters. Position 13 red mini M&M's and fruit allsorts quarters on body. Use the fruit ring halves to make the frill around clown's neck.

9 Cut a strip of red bootlace for mouth; position on face. Secure blue mini M&M's to peppermints with a little butter cream; position on head for eyes. Trim freckle to make hat; position remaining red mini M&M's at base of hat. Secure red Smartie on top of hat with a little butter cream.

10 Cut green sour strap into strips to make hair; top hands with small pink jelly beans to make fingers. Tie two 20cm pieces of red bootlace into bows; position for shoelaces.

11 Using star cutter, cut four stars from yellow layer of remaining fruit allsort; position on balls.

tip There will be about ⅔ cup of the cake mixture left, enough to make 10 more balls to share with the juggler's guests.

pans&equipment

1   round fluted cutter
2   round cutter
3   3.5cm duck cutter
4   12cm star cutter
5   6-hole (¾-cup/180ml) texas muffin pan
6   texas muffin paper cases
7   8-hole (½-cup/125ml) mini loaf pan
8   12-hole (1-tablespoon/20ml)
    shallow-based patty pan
9   12-hole (1-tablespoon/20ml)
    mini muffin pan
10 mini muffin paper cases
11 deep 20cm-round cake pan
12 9-hole (½-cup/125ml) friand pan
13 fluted pastry wheel
14 2.5-litre (10-cup) dolly varden pan
15 deep 23cm-square cake pan
16 2.25-litre (9-cup) pudding steamer
17 12-hole (2-tablespoons/40ml)
    deep flat-based patty pan
18 standard paper cases
19 12-hole (⅓-cup/80ml) standard
    muffin pan
20 plastic chocolate mould
21 20cm x 30cm lamington pan

1 Use foil or other grease-repelling paper for covering cake boards or, if using a non-grease-repelling paper, cover it with a clear adhesive product that will stop the icing from staining the paper. For round and oval boards, trace around the board on the back of the paper, cut the paper about 2cm outside the traced line. Snip the paper, almost up to the traced line, then fold and paste the snipped edges onto the board.

4 Melted butter is traditionally used for greasing cake pans. Use a brush to coat the surface of the pan evenly, however, you can also use your fingers, as they will spread the melted butter more evenly than the brush.

5 Round, and square cake pans with rounded corners, can be lined in the same way. Cut a strip of baking or greaseproof paper about 5cm wider than the side of the pan, fold a 2cm band over, and snip the paper in the same way as step 1. Fit the paper around the side(s) and base of the pan. If using baking paper, grease the pan first to hold the paper in position. Greaseproof paper is less rigid, and will fit into the pan without being greased first.

basic-know-how

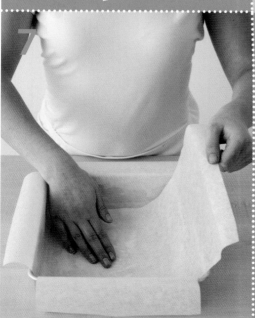

7 Some cake pans only need to be lined with strips of baking or greaseproof paper, this is often for insulation or for making the removal of the cake from the pan easier. It is always best to grease the pan before lining with paper strips, not only to hold the paper securely in place, but to make sure the cooked cake will easily come away from the corners of the pan. Simply criss-cross strips of paper long and wide enough to cover the base and sides of the pan with an over hang of paper.

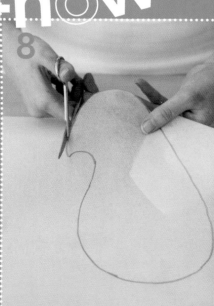

2 Square boards are quicker and easier to cover than round boards. Trace the shape of the board on the back of the paper (see step 1 for best type of paper to use); cut the paper 2cm outside the traced line. Neatly fold the corners over and paste (or use tape) to the back of the board. If the paper is bulky, snip off a corner of the paper (as if covering a book). Boards can be made from craft wood, Masonite, or heavy card, or can be bought, already covered, from cake decorating supply shops.

3 Greasing cake pans properly is important. Use a cooking-oil spray; shake the can of spray well before you use it and make sure it is applied evenly all over the surface of the pan. Cake pans that have a non-stick coating need to be greased lightly and evenly, especially if the coating has been scratched – this is where the cake mixture will almost certainly stick.

6 Trace the base of the pan onto a piece of baking or greaseproof paper; cut out the shape slightly inside the traced line to be sure the base lining fits inside the pan – this allows for the thickness of the paper as well as the thickness of the pan.

8 There are patterns for various cakes and accompaniments in the back of this book. To use them, trace the pattern or template you need onto greaseproof or baking paper, then cut out the shape using sharp scissors.

9 Secure the paper pattern to the cake – usually the base of the cake, but be guided by individual recipes – with strong pointed toothpicks. Use a sharp pointed vegetable knife to cut out the cake shape evenly, keeping the sides of the cake as straight as possible. Freeze the cake while preparing the icing; the freezing process will help hold the cake crumbs in position when the icing is applied to cut surfaces.

10

10 Butter cream is the most commonly used icing in this book. Use butter at room temperature, or slightly softened, not melted. Beat the butter in a small bowl with an electric mixer until it is as white as possible. Warm the bowl and beaters under hot water before mixing if the room temperature is cold. The use of a small bowl will ensure that the beaters are well down into the mixture to create the correct texture and volume. The picture shows butter before and after beating.

13 It can be quite tricky to make the surface of the butter cream appear smooth after it has been applied to the cake. Have a glass of hot water nearby while applying the icing; dip the blade of a small metal spatula into the hot water, dry the hot blade, then quickly spread and smooth the butter cream over the cake's surface. Repeat this heating and drying as the blade cools down.

13

14 Small dabs of butter cream will join cakes together, secure cakes to prepared boards, and secure small decorations and lollies to cakes. The butter cream doesn't set and dry, but it will hold things in place well enough.

16

16 Knead colouring into ready-made white icing starting with the tiniest amount possible; test the strength of the colouring on a small piece of icing. Work on a surface that has been dusted lightly with sifted icing sugar. Pure icing sugar is best to use for dusting, but it's not essential unless the recipe specifies. Gently work and knead the colouring through the icing until it's evenly coloured. The icing should have lost any stickiness, but shouldn't be dry. Keep the icing covered, away from the air.

17

11 Once the butter cream
is as white as possible, beat in the
sifted icing sugar and milk, in about
four batches. The butter cream will
become light and fluffy during the
beating process. Plain butter cream
is a cream colour, not white.

12 Use the best quality food
colourings you can find: the best are
from cake decorating supply shops –
they are relatively expensive, but are
highly concentrated, come in a huge
range of colours and will last for years.
These colourings will give you bold
colours, like red and black: just keep
beating the colouring into the butter
cream until you get the depth of
colour you want. When tinting pale
pink, butter cream may appear to
be an apricot or salmon colour.

15 When fluffy frosting is
first applied to a cake it is like
marshmallow, then it sets and
resembles meringue. It's important to
boil the syrup to the right stage; it
should be thick, but not coloured. Add
the syrup, in a thin steady stream, to
the egg whites while they're being
beaten in a small bowl for maximum
volume. Use a spatula for spreading
the frosting over the cake.

17 Ready-made white icing
is easy to use; it will cover whole
cakes or just their tops, giving a
smooth finish. It can be shaped
and moulded into all sorts of things,
from rope to roses, in this book it
is mostly used as a covering or cut
into various shapes, such as letters
and numbers. The icing is usually
rolled to a specified thickness,
either on a board or on baking
paper, then the shapes are cut out
and left to dry completely, usually
flat, for several hours.

18 Flowers made from
marshmallows are a favourite
stand-by for cake decorations. Snip
the marshmallows in half horizontally
using sharp scissors – the scissors
squash the halves into an oval shape
after snipping – then gently pinch the
ends of each half into a petal shape.
If the marshmallow sticks to your
fingertips, dip them in a little icing
sugar or cornflour.

19

19 Piping bags are especially useful if you're using a lot of different coloured icings; they're easy to make and are disposable, whereas the bags made from various fabrics need washing and drying before you can use them again. Cut a square from baking paper (it's stronger than greaseproof paper), then cut it diagonally into two triangles. Hold the apex of the triangle towards you, and roll the paper into a cone shape by bringing the three points of the triangle together.

20

22 Break or chop the chocolate into pieces and put it into a china or glass bowl; stand the bowl over a saucepan of a size that will hold the bowl, and that contains enough simmering water to create steam under the bowl (the water must not touch the bottom of the bowl). Stir the chocolate gently over a medium heat until it is smooth; remove the bowl from the pan immediately. Water must not come into contact with the chocolate or it will seize and be unusable.

22

23 Melting chocolate in a microwave oven works well, but it needs constant checking. Microwave ovens vary in strength, so melt a few pieces of chocolate in your oven first to assess its melting ability. Spread pieces of chocolate, in a single layer, onto a microwave-safe plate; be guided by the instruction booklet for the right setting and a rough idea of timing. The pieces of chocolate will hold their shape, even after they have melted; check it's been melted properly.

25

25 Colouring caster or regular crystal sugar (or jelly crystals or coconut) is easy and less messy if it's done in a strong plastic bag. Add a drop or two of colouring to the sugar in the bag, close the bag, then massage the colouring evenly through the sugar. Add another drop of colouring if you need a stronger colour.

26

20 Staple the bag together just below where the three points meet – adhesive tape won't stick to baking paper. Fill the bag, about three-quarters full (or less), with icing, then fold the stapled end over the icing; fold the sides over to enclose the icing in the bag.

21 Disposable plastic piping bags are available in some supermarkets and cake decorating supply shops; use these the same way you would use paper piping bags. Once the bag is about three-quarters full, use sharp scissors to snip the tiniest amount from the piping end of the bag – you can always snip more off the end if it's not enough the first time around. Practice piping with the bag before you start on the cake, it's surprisingly easy.

24 Licorice straps have been used a lot in this book for various cake decorations. Often we have used long or short strips for the finishing touches to cakes. Use small sharp scissors to cut strips of the required lengths from the straps.

26 Sugar, jelly crystals or coconut can be coloured in a bowl if you prefer; wear disposable gloves when working the colouring through the sugar, otherwise you will have colouring on your fingertips for many days.

27 Pressing hundreds and thousands, coconut, nuts, etc., onto the sides of cakes can be messy. If the cake is of a shape and size (large or small, it doesn't matter) that it can be lifted and handled easily, then spread the sides (not the tops) with the icing. Roll the sides of the cakes in the hundreds and thousands, then ice the tops of the cakes. Place the hundreds and thousands into a shallow dish for easy rolling.

1

1 Larry lion (page 8)

Cut a 1cm slice from the bottom of each small cake. The large pieces of the cakes are used to make the lion's mane; eight of the slices from the cakes are used to make the features on the lion's face. The remaining 10 slices of cake are not used.

2

4 Use a small sharp, finely serrated knife to trim the cake to a teardrop shape to make the echidna.

4

5 Use a small sharp, finely serrated knife to trim the cake to an oval shape for the wombat. Trim and round two opposite sides of the cakes to minimise the cut area.

step-by-step

7

7 Caterpillar (page 14)

Use a small sharp pointed knife to cut a small crescent-shape from each cake that represents a segment of the caterpillar; this is to make the segments fit snugly together.

2 The picture shows how the eight 1cm slices for the lion's nose should be stacked to make his features. Spread the slices with butter cream, top with the sprinkles, then position each cake as shown.

3

3 **Bush buddies (page 10)** Use a small sharp, finely serrated knife to trim the cake to a more rounded shape for the cockatoo. This step can also be used to make rounded shapes for the following cakes: *Taffy turtle (page 84); Snow folk (page 149).*

5

6 **Cheeky frogs in a pond (page 13)** Use a small sharp pointed knife to cut a wedge-shape from each biscuit to make the lily pads for the frogs.

6

8 **Smiley starfish (page 18)** It's important to secure cakes to the board or plate etc., especially where a lot of small cakes are used, as in Smiley Starfish. A small dab of butter cream (or any of the other icings used in this book) should be spread onto the bottom of each cake – large or small – before it is positioned on the board.

9

9 **Felicity fish (page 21)** To make the fish shape, trace and cut out the pattern for the body, tail and fins from the pattern sheet provided. Attach the pattern of the fish's body to the cake with strong pointed wooden toothpicks; cut around the curve and down 1cm into the cake. Using a large serrated knife, slice the piece of cake away, 1cm from the top of the cake – in one piece – as shown. The fins and tail are then cut from this 1cm layer of cake (see steps 10 & 11, page 168).

10

10
Picture shows the shaped body of the fish at the back, and the cut away 1cm-thick slice at the front.

11

13
Flower bouquet (page 37)
The cakes need to be secured to the styrofoam ball with strong wooden pointed toothpicks, pushed about halfway into the ball and about halfway into the base of each cake. Either have someone help to do this, or stand the ball in a stable tall jug with the chopstick in the jug. The cake can be handed to the birthday girl, or displayed on the party table like a posy.

13

14
Princess Belinda (page 49)
First position one band of the cakes around the bottom of the skirt, then position the next band of cakes, placing each cake between two cakes on the bottom band as you work your way up the skirt. This won't always be possible without leaving gaps. The bottom two bands will do the work of supporting the top bands.

16

16
Magic wands (page 52)
Use a sharp metal 12cm star-shaped cutter (the cutter was measured at its longest point) to cut out the stars. It doesn't matter if the stars are cut from the top or the bottom of the cake; it's important to get as good a star shape as possible.

17

11 Attach the patterns for the ~~t~~ail and fins to the slice of cake using ~~s~~trong wooden pointed toothpicks. ~~U~~se a small sharp, finely serrated ~~k~~nife to cut out the shapes.

12

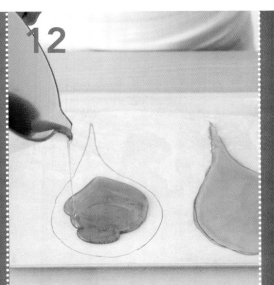

12 Buzzy bee (page 32)
Using the pattern sheet provided, trace two wings onto baking paper, turn the paper upside down onto a flat heatproof surface, like a wooden board or oven tray. After the bubbles have subsided in the toffee, pour the toffee slowly over the wing outlines. Leave toffee to set at room temperature. Position the wings just before the party.

14

15 Glambags (page 50)
Use a small sharp, finely serrated knife to trim long sides from loaf cakes on an angle, leaving a small flat area on top of each cake; discard trimmings.

15

17 Heart balloons (page 55)
Cut a segment from each friand. Join the two cut segments together with a toothpick to form heart shapes. The toothpick will be hidden inside the iced cake, so be sure to remove it before giving the cake to children to eat.

18

18 Cute cottages (page 56)
Turn each cake for the roofs top-side down; use a small sharp, finely serrated knife to trim four sides from each cake, keeping a small area on top of the cakes flat. The cake on the right of the picture shows the assembled cottage before icing.

19

19 **Fiery dragon (page 58)**
Use a small sharp, finely serrated knife to trim one end of a friand so that the other two friands sit snugly together for the dragon's head.

20

22 **Paint pots (page 92).**
Use the round cutter to mark and cut through the top of each cake to a depth of about 1.5cm. Carefully scoop out the cake and discard, making room for the "paint" to be poured into the hole. This step can also be used for the *Tea party (page 82)* cake; use the round cutter to mark and cut through the top of each cake to a depth of about 4cm. Carefully scoop out the cake and discard, rnaking room for the "tea" to be poured into the hole.

22

23 **Taffy turtle (page 84)**
Using paper pattern and a small sharp, finely serrated knife, cut a hexagonal shape from the centre of the pudding-shaped cake. Cut out the rest of the body shape by cutting pieces from each point of the hexagon outwards.

25

25 **Sunny umbrella (page 95)**
Using paper pattern from pattern sheet, and a small sharp, finely serrated knife, cut out umbrella shape. Secure to prepared board with a little butter cream. Reserve remaining cake.

2

20 Good ship (page 76)
Using the paper pattern for the ship, cut out the shape using a small sharp, finely serrated knife. Trim around the front side of the ship to make it rounded, including the hull, bow and stern.

21 Fishbowl fun (page 81)
Using paper pattern, cut out the shape of the fishbowl. Secure the cake to the prepared board with a little butter cream. Use the blue butter cream for water, make some ripples in the water, then spread the top of the cake with white butter cream.

24 Using paper pattern for turtle's flippers, attach the pattern to one of the loaf cakes. Using a small sharp, finely serrated knife, cut out the flipper shape. Repeat with remaining loaf cakes to make four flippers.

26 Using a sharp metal 3cm-round cutter, cut out eight rounds from the reserved cake to make the umbrella's handle. We used a 5cm-deep cutter, to make cutting right through the cake easier.

27 Yo-yos (page 107)
Shape and press each round of kneaded and rolled icing over the rounded bottoms of the cakes that have been brushed with warmed, sieved apricot jam. Tuck a little of the icing over the edges of the cakes, as shown in the picture at left. Keep the icing that you're not using covered, to keep it from drying out while you make the yo-yos one at a time.

28

28 Hopscotch (page 118)

Turn cake top-side down; use a large sharp serrated knife to trim all the sides of the cake to a neat rectangle measuring 14cm x 28cm.

29

31 Use a small sharp knife to gently mark vertical lines onto the cupcake "bases", don't cut all the way through the icing. Position on the cupcakes, just barely covering the edges of the cupcake "tops".

31

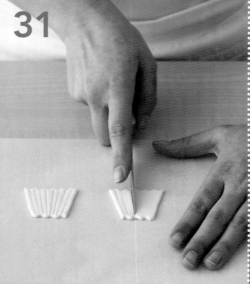

32 Number 2 (page 126)

Use the handle of a teaspoon to make a small hole in the top of the cake. Push the sour worms into the cake, as shown. This step can also be used to create worm holes for the *Number 6* cake *(page 134)*.

34

34 Crazy clowns (page 152)

Using a 4cm cutter, mark a round on each of the four cakes in the paper cases. Using a small sharp pointed vegetable knife, cut into each cake, on an angle and to a depth of about 2cm, to make the clowns' hats.

35

29 Using paper pattern sheet and a small sharp, finely serrated knife, cut "home" cake from one narrow end of the trimmed cake. Cut the remaining cake neatly into eight 7cm squares. Picture shows "home" cake and a piece of the remaining cake before it is cut.

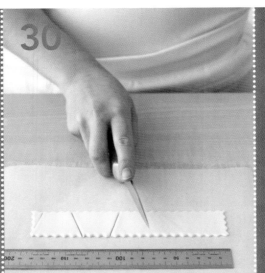

30 Number 4 (page 130)

Working with one piece of kneaded coloured ready-made icing at a time, use a rolling pin to roll each piece between pieces of baking paper (or on a surface dusted with sifted icing sugar) to a strip about 4cm x 19cm long. Use a ruler and a fluted pastry wheel to cut the strip into a 3cm x 18cm rectangle. Use a small sharp knife to cut the strip into the "bases" for the cupcakes.

33 Number 7 (page 137);

Heat a small metal spatula under very hot water (dry the blade before using it). Gently press the hot blade against the side of an after-dinner mint to melt the chocolate. Quickly press another mint against the melted chocolate to make the tent. The chocolate will re-set very quickly. If you make a mistake, break the mints apart and repeat the process. This step can also be used to make the bridge on the *Number 8* cake (*page 138*).

35 Turn the cakes, without paper cases, top-side down; use a small sharp, finely serrated knife to trim the cakes into rounded shapes. This step can also be used to make rounded shapes for the following cakes: *Cheeky frogs in a pond (page 13); Baby bluebirds (page 17); Ladybirds (page 22); Buzzy bee (page 32); Ice-cream cones (page 96).*

36 Push a metal or wooden skewer into both sides of the clowns' heads to make about 12 holes on each cake for the hair. Gently push single pieces of sugar-coated bootlace into the holes. The cakes can be completely decorated, just leaving the hair to do, about an hour before the party.

lollies

1   jubes
2   mini musk lollies
3   mini rainbow musk lollies
4   jelly beans
5   small round lollipops
6   round peppermints
7   jelly babies
8   mint leaves
9   snakes
10 Killer Python
11 Mallow Bakes
12 giant marshmallows
13 regular marshmallows
14 BoPeep lollies
15 fruit rings
16 large fruit rings
17 conversation hearts
18 bananas
19 fruit sticks
20 musk sticks
21 TicTacs
22 strawberries and creams
23 Life Savers
24 lolly doughnuts
25 sugar-coated red licorice bootlace
26 sugar-coated blue licorice bootlace
27 fizzers
28 red and green sour strap
29 rainbow sour strap
30 red and blue sour strap
31 sour worms
32 black licorice bootlace
33 red licorice bootlace
34 black licorice rope
35 black licorice strap
36 red licorice strap
37 "Double D" sugar-free drop lollies
38 candy orange wedges
39 licorice allsorts
40 fruit allsorts

The lollies used in this book are just a guide;
use similar ones, or use any lollies you like, or
that are available in your area – the results will
be just as delicious. All the lollies used in this
book were available at the time of printing.

decorations

1   freckles
2   giant milk-chocolate freckle
3   scorched peanuts
4   clinkers
5   gold- and silver-foil wrapped
    chocolate coins
6   foil-wrapped chocolate fish
7   foil-wrapped chocolate ladybirds
8   Raffaello white chocolate balls
9   gold- and silver-foil wrapped
    chocolate hearts
10 foil-wrapped chocolate eggs
11 solid milk chocolate eggs
12 candy-coated speckled chocolate eggs
13 grissini bread sticks
14 large cream-filled chocolate biscuits
15 small cream-filled chocolate biscuits
16 chocolate malt sticks
17 plain chocolate biscuits
18 digestive biscuits
19 Milk Arrowroot biscuits
20 chocolate finger biscuits
21 chocolate lamington finger
22 chocolate lamington
23 after-dinner mints, square-shaped
24 Curly Wurly bar
25 after-dinner mints, stick-shaped
26 Cherry Ripe bar
27 POCO wafer sticks
28 large double red icing heart
29 ice-cream wafers
30 square-bottom ice-cream cones
31 Violet Crumble bar
32 Flake bar
33 dark chocolate Melts
34 milk chocolate Toblerone bar
35 white Choc Bits
36 Maltesers
37 silver cachous
38 pearl cachous
39 mixed cachous
40 edible icing flowers
41 edible icing butterfly
42 edible glitter
43 decorating gel
44 hundreds and thousands
45 sugar crystals
46 sprinkles
47 candy heart sprinkles
48 rainbow choc-chips
49 mini M&M's
50 M&M's
51 Jaffas
52 Smarties

baking info

We have used cakes made from packet mixes throughout this book for consistency of size and baking times. We used 470g packets, however, there are other sizes available and they will all work with our recipes.

If you want to make your own cakes, choose any of the recipes on page 179; they will all bake at similar temperatures, times, and in the same pan sizes as the packet mix cakes suggested in each recipe. One quantity of any of the cake recipes is equivalent to one 470g packet cake mix. Here are some extra tips to help you make beautiful cakes for each and every birthday party.

Beating
It's important to beat the packet mixes properly using an electric mixer – not a food processor or blender. We found a stand-alone mixer gave us the best results, simply because it's easier to let the machine do the work rather than holding a hand-held mixer (there is a tendency to under-beat the mixture using one of these). Also, it's important to beat the packet mixes enough to develop the volume of the mixture. Have the ingredients to be added at room temperature for the best results, start the mixer at a low speed to incorporate the ingredients, then gradually increase the speed to medium. As a rule, one packet of cake mix fits into a small bowl, two or three packets into a medium bowl, and four packets into a large bowl. The beaters should always be well down in the mixture to create volume.

Measuring
To achieve the same results (in terms of numbers and sizes) as we did of the cakes in this book, it's important to measure the mixture accurately into the correct-sized cake pans. We've indicated the fluid capacity of the pans we've used in each recipe; it's worth checking this before you start. Often there is some cake mixture left over,

just use it to make more cakes for the party. Some of the cakes in this book require half-packets of cake mixture to be used, weigh or measure the contents to make sure they're halved accurately. Make sure you halve the ingredients indicated on the packet to get the balance of the mixture correct. Make the whole packet mixture if you like, then simply make more cakes for the party, they'll never go amiss.

Cake pans
There are two sizes of patty pans used in this book, standard and deep flat-based. You'll notice they have different fluid capacities, but both still hold the standard-sized paper cases. We've also used texas and mini muffin pans with similar-sized paper cases to fit their capacity, and friand and mini loaf pans. All of these pans are available in supermarkets, kitchen, department and chain stores. The quality and finish vary; most have a non-stick coating, but we grease them anyway. Some of the recipes need a large cake to be made first, then that cake is cut into smaller shapes; we used good quality, straight-sided aluminium cake pans for the larger cakes. Cake pans made from stainless steel, tin, anodised metals or metals with non-stick coatings, conduct heat differently from aluminium; cakes made in these pans need to be baked 10°C lower in temperature than those baked in uncoated aluminium pans.

Paper cases
We used a variety of shapes, sizes and colours in this book; often we matched the cake's icings and/or decorations to the paper cases. The cases are available in supermarkets, specialty kitchen shops, department and chain stores, cake decorating supply shops and homeware shops. Sometimes small baked (patty/muffin) cakes will shrink away from the paper cases as they cool. To help prevent this, cool the cakes slowly by covering them with a cloth, and keeping them away from draughts, fans or air-conditioners.

Baking
If you need to bake more than two trays of cakes, the cake mixture (either packet or homemade) will keep well at a cool room temperature for up to an hour. Fan-forced ovens should bake everything that is being cooked in the oven evenly, however, some domestic ovens have hot spots, and it will be necessary to change the positions of the cakes about halfway through the baking time. It's fine to cook more than one cake on the same oven rack, but the cake pans shouldn't touch each other or the sides of the oven or the closed oven door. It's usually a good idea to change the positions of the cake pans on the same rack, too. Remember that cakes rise, allow for this when positioning the racks before the oven is preheated. As a guide, cakes should be baked in the centre of the oven, more towards the lower half of the oven. If the oven is loaded with cakes of varying sizes, they might take a little longer to bake than our recipes indicate.

Pattern sheet
This is at the back of the book; the patterns are actual size. Trace them onto a piece of baking paper, then cut out.

Food colourings
Use good quality colourings for the best results; they will "hold" the colour in the icing. Some of the inexpensive liquid colourings will fade or darken the icing on standing. Icings or frostings based on butter are the most difficult to colour as butter is yellow, so any colour will be affected by the base colour. This is why it's important to beat the butter until it's as white as possible. Fluffy frosting and royal icing are the easiest to colour, because they're white to begin with. Coloured icings can change on standing, particularly if you're using liquid colourings. If possible (it's not with fluffy frosting), colour a small portion of the icing to the shade you want, keep it airtight, and let it stand for a few hours before colouring the whole batch.

cake recipes

Basic buttercake
125g butter, softened
½ teaspoon vanilla extract
¾ cup (165g) caster sugar
2 eggs
1½ cups (225g) self-raising flour
½ cup (125ml) milk

Preheat oven. Grease (and line) pan(s). Beat butter, extract and sugar in small bowl with electric mixer until light and fluffy. Beat in eggs, one at a time. Stir in sifted flour and milk, in two batches. Bake as directed.

To marble a butter cake, place portions of cake mixture in three bowls then tint each with the desired colour. Drop spoonfuls of mixture into pan(s), alternating colours, then swirl together with a skewer for a marbled effect.

Quick chocolate cake
1⅓ cups (200g) self-raising flour
½ cup (50g) cocoa powder
125g butter, softened
½ teaspoon vanilla extract
1¼ cups (275g) caster sugar
2 eggs
⅔ cup (160ml) water

Preheat oven. Grease (and line) pan(s). Sift flour and cocoa into medium bowl, add remaining ingredients; beat on low speed with electric mixer until ingredients are combined. Increase speed to medium; beat about 3 minutes or until mixture is smooth and changed to a lighter colour. Bake as directed.

Carrot cake
½ cup (125ml) vegetable oil
2 eggs
¾ cup (110g) self-raising flour
½ cup (110g) firmly packed brown sugar
2 teaspoons mixed spice
1½ cups (360g) firmly packed coarsely grated carrot

Preheat oven. Grease (and line) pan(s). Combine oil, eggs, sifted flour, sugar and spice in medium bowl; stir in carrot. Bake as directed.

Gluten-free carrot cake
1 cup (125g) soy or besan (chickpea) flour
¾ cup (110g) cornflour (100% corn)
2 teaspoons gluten-free baking powder
1 teaspoon bicarbonate of soda
2 teaspoons mixed spice
1 cup (220g) firmly packed brown sugar
1 cup (120g) coarsely chopped roasted walnuts
1½ cups (360g) coarsely grated carrot
½ cup (125ml) extra light olive oil
½ cup (120g) sour cream
3 eggs

Preheat oven. Grease (and line) pan(s). Sift flours, baking powder, soda and spice into large bowl; stir in sugar, nuts and carrot. Stir in combined oil, sour cream and eggs. Bake as directed.

Gluten-free cupcakes
125g butter, softened
2 teaspoons finely grated lemon rind
¾ cup (165g) caster sugar
4 eggs
2 cups (240g) almond meal
½ cup (40g) desiccated coconut
½ cup (100g) rice flour
1 teaspoon bicarbonate of soda

Preheat oven. Grease (and line) pan(s). Beat butter, rind and sugar in small bowl with electric mixer until light and fluffy. Beat in eggs one at a time (mixture will separate at this stage); transfer mixture to a large bowl. Stir in almond meal, coconut then sifted flour and soda. Bake as directed.

White chocolate mud cake
165g butter, chopped coarsely
100g white eating chocolate, chopped coarsely
1 cup (220g) caster sugar
⅔ cup (160ml) milk
1 cup (150g) plain flour
⅓ cup (50g) self-raising flour
1 egg

Preheat oven. Grease (and line) pan(s). Combine butter, chocolate, sugar and milk in medium saucepan; stir over low heat until smooth. Cool 30 minutes. Whisk in sifted flours, then egg. Bake as directed.

Dark chocolate mud cake
225g butter, chopped coarsely
360g dark chocolate, chopped coarsely
¾ cup (165g) firmly packed brown sugar
¾ cup (180ml) water
1 cup (150g) plain flour
¼ cup (35g) self-raising flour
2 tablespoons cocoa powder
2 eggs

Preheat oven. Grease (and line) pan(s). Combine butter, chocolate, sugar and the water in medium saucepan; stir over low heat until smooth. Cool 30 minutes. Whisk in sifted flours and cocoa then eggs. Bake as directed.

icing recipes

Butter cream

Basic butter cream is also known as vienna cream; the flavour can be varied by adding any essence you like (see *basic know-how numbers 10-14*, pages 162-163).

125g butter, softened
1½ cups (240g) icing sugar
2 tablespoons milk

Beat butter in small bowl with electric mixer until as white as possible. Gradually beat in half the sifted icing sugar, milk, then remaining icing sugar.

Chocolate variation

Sift ⅓ cup (35g) cocoa powder in with the first batch of icing sugar.

Glacé icing

2¼ cups (360g) icing sugar
¼ cup (60ml) water
food colouring

1 Sift icing sugar into a small heatproof bowl, stir in enough water to give a firm paste. Colour as desired. Stir the paste over a small saucepan of hot water (the water should not touch the bottom of the bowl) until icing is spreadable; do not overheat. The bottom of the bowl should feel warm (not hot) to the touch.

Fluffy mock cream frosting

2 tablespoons milk
⅓ cup (80ml) water
1 cup (220g) caster sugar
1 teaspoon gelatine
2 tablespoons water, extra
250g butter, softened
1 teaspoon vanilla extract

1 Combine milk, the water and sugar in small saucepan; stir over low heat, without boiling, until sugar is dissolved.

2 Sprinkle gelatine over the extra water in a cup, add to pan; stir sugar syrup until gelatine is dissolved. Cool to room temperature.

3 Beat butter and extract in small bowl with electric mixer until as white as possible. While motor is operating, gradually pour in cold syrup, in a thin steady stream; beat until light and fluffy. Mixture will thicken more on standing.

Fluffy frosting

1 cup (220g) caster sugar
⅓ cup (80ml) water
2 egg whites

1 Combine sugar and the water in small saucepan; stir with a wooden spoon over high heat, without boiling, until sugar dissolves. Boil, uncovered, without stirring, about 3 to 5 minutes or until syrup is slightly thick. If a candy thermometer is available, the syrup will be ready when it reaches 114°C (240°F).

2 When the syrup is thick, remove the pan from the heat, allow the bubbles to subside then test the syrup by dropping 1 teaspoon into a cup of cold water. The syrup should form a ball of soft sticky toffee. The syrup should not be changed in colour; if it has, it has been cooked for too long and you will have to discard it and start again.

3 While the syrup is boiling (see step 1), and after about four minutes, beat the egg whites in a small bowl with an electric mixer until stiff; keep beating (or the whites will deflate) until syrup reaches the correct temperature.

4 When syrup is ready, allow bubbles to subside then pour a very thin stream onto the egg whites with mixer operating on medium speed. If the syrup is added too quickly to the egg whites the frosting will not thicken.

5 Continue beating and adding syrup until all syrup is used. Continue to beat until frosting stands in stiff peaks (frosting should be barely warm).

6 For best results, frosting should be applied to a cake on the day it is to be served. While you can frost the cake the day before, the frosting will become crisp and lose its glossy appearance, much like a meringue (see *basic know-how number 15*, page 163).

Ready-made white icing

This is available from cake-decorating suppliers and some health-food shops, delicatessens and supermarkets. There are several brands available, and they can be sold as Soft Icing, Prepared Icing or Ready-to-Roll Icing. This is very easy to use. Break off as much icing as you need; re-wrap remaining icing to exclude the air, or a crust will develop, which will spoil the smooth texture of the icing.

Knead the piece of icing on a surface lightly dusted with sifted icing sugar (see *basic know-how numbers 16-17*, pages 162-163). If colouring the icing, start working tiny amounts of the colouring through the icing. The icing should be smooth and free from stickiness. Only work with small amounts of icing at the one time as the air will dry it out. Cover any rolled-out icing with plastic wrap.

Royal icing

1½ cups (240g) pure icing sugar
1 egg white
½ teaspoon lemon juice

1 Sift icing sugar through very fine sieve. Lightly beat egg white in a small bowl with an electric mixer; add icing sugar, a tablespoon at a time. When icing reaches firm peaks, use a wooden spoon to beat in the juice. Royal icing must be kept covered, either with a well wrung out wet cloth then plastic wrap, or with the plastic wrap pressed onto the surface of the icing. Royal icing develops a crust when it's left open to the air – this usually makes the icing unusable, particularly for piping.

glossary

almond meal also known as ground almonds; nuts are powdered to a coarse flour texture for use in baking.

baking powder a raising agent consisting mainly of two parts cream of tartar to one part bicarbonate of soda (baking soda). Gluten-free baking powder is made without cereals.

bicarbonate of soda also known as baking soda; used as a leavening agent in baking.

biscuits
Milk Arrowroot a plain biscuit that was launched in 1888 and has been a staple for Australian families ever since. It contained arrowroot, a common source of starch, and was seen as a good, easily digestible, food for young children.
chocolate finger long thin finger-shaped biscuit covered in chocolate.
chocolate malt sticks thin finger-shaped malt biscuit covered in chocolate. Shorter than a chocolate finger biscuit.
digestive wheatmeal biscuit with a soft, crunchy, buttery texture.

butter use salted or unsalted (sweet) butter; 125g is equal to one stick (4 ounces) of butter.

chenille sticks also known as pipe cleaners; available from craft stores.

chocolate
choc Bits also known as chocolate chips or chocolate morsels; available in milk, white and dark chocolate.
Melts small discs of compounded milk, white or dark chocolate; ideal for melting and moulding.
dark eating also known as semi-sweet or luxury chocolate.
milk eating most popular eating chocolate; mild and very sweet.
white eating contains no cocoa solids but derives its sweet flavour from cocoa butter. Is very sensitive to heat.

Ice Magic a chocolate flavouring that sets within seconds after being poured over cold desserts.

cocoa powder also called cocoa; unsweetened, dried, roasted then ground cocoa beans.

coconut
desiccated unsweetened, concentrated, dried, finely shredded coconut.
shredded thin strips of dried coconut.

cream
fresh also known as pure cream and pouring cream.
sour a thick commercially-cultured soured cream.
thickened a whipping cream containing a thickener.

cream of tartar the acid ingredient in baking powder; when added to confectionery mixtures it helps prevent sugar from crystallising. Keeps frostings creamy, and improves the volume when beating egg whites.

flour
besan also known as chickpea flour or gram; made from ground chickpeas so is gluten-free and high in protein.
cornflour also known as cornstarch; used as a thickening agent in cooking.
plain all-purpose flour made from wheat.
rice very fine, almost powdery, gluten-free flour; made from ground white rice.
self-raising plain flour combined with baking powder in the proportion of 1 cup flour to 2 teaspoons baking powder.
soy made from roasted soya beans ground into a fine powder.

gelatine we use powdered gelatine. It is also available in sheet form, known as leaf gelatine.

glossy decorating gel prepared icing available in different colours; comes in a tube with a small nozzle and used mainly to add outlines and other details.

jelly crystals a powdered mixture of gelatine, sweetener and artificial fruit flavouring used to make a moulded, translucent, quivering dessert. Also known as jello.

lamington pan 20cm x 30cm slab cake pan, 3cm deep.

lollies a confectionery also known as sweets or candy.

macadamia a rich, buttery nut native to Australia; store in refrigerator because of its high oil content.

maple syrup a thin syrup distilled from the sap of the maple tree. Maple-flavoured syrup or pancake syrup is not an adequate substitute for the real thing.

milk we use full-cream milk.

mixed spice a blend of ground spices usually consisting of cinnamon, allspice and nutmeg.

sugar
caster also known as superfine or finely granulated table sugar.
brown a soft, finely granulated sugar retaining molasses for its characteristic colour and flavour.
demerara golden coloured granulated sugar with a distinctive rich flavour that is often favoured by coffee drinkers.
icing sugar also known as confectioners' sugar or powdered sugar; granulated sugar crushed together with a small amount of cornflour.
pure icing sugar also known as confectioners' sugar or powdered sugar; granulated sugar crushed without the addition of cornflour.
white a coarse, white granulated table sugar, also known as crystal sugar.

sultanas dried grapes; also known as golden raisins.

vanilla extract obtained from vanilla beans infused in water.

conversion chart

measures

One Australian metric measuring cup holds approximately 250ml; one Australian metric tablespoon holds 20ml; one Australian metric teaspoon holds 5ml.

The difference between one country's measuring cups and another's is within a two- or three-teaspoon variance, and will not affect your cooking results. North America, New Zealand and the United Kingdom use a 15ml tablespoon.

All cup and spoon measurements are level. The most accurate way of measuring dry ingredients is to weigh them. When measuring liquids, use a clear glass or plastic jug with the metric markings.

We use large eggs with an average weight of 60g.

dry measures

METRIC	IMPERIAL
15g	½oz
30g	1oz
60g	2oz
90g	3oz
125g	4oz (¼lb)
155g	5oz
185g	6oz
220g	7oz
250g	8oz (½lb)
280g	9oz
315g	10oz
345g	11oz
375g	12oz (¾lb)
410g	13oz
440g	14oz
470g	15oz
500g	16oz (1lb)
750g	24oz (1½lb)
1kg	32oz (2lb)

liquid measures

METRIC	IMPERIAL
30ml	1 fluid oz
60ml	2 fluid oz
100ml	3 fluid oz
125ml	4 fluid oz
150ml	5 fluid oz (¼ pint/1 gill)
190ml	6 fluid oz
250ml	8 fluid oz
300ml	10 fluid oz (½ pint)
500ml	16 fluid oz
600ml	20 fluid oz (1 pint)
1000ml (1 litre)	1¾ pints

length measures

METRIC	IMPERIAL
3mm	⅛ in
6mm	¼in
1cm	½in
2cm	¾in
2.5cm	1in
5cm	2in
6cm	2½in
8cm	3in
10cm	4in
13cm	5in
15cm	6in
18cm	7in
20cm	8in
23cm	9in
25cm	10in
28cm	11in
30cm	12in (1ft)

oven temperatures

These oven temperatures are only a guide for conventional ovens. For fan-forced ovens, check the manufacturer's manual.

	°C (CELSIUS)	°F (FAHRENHEIT)	GAS MARK
Very slow	120	250	½
Slow	150	275-300	1-2
Moderately slow	160	325	3
Moderate	180	350-375	4-5
Moderately hot	200	400	6
Hot	220	425-450	7-8
Very hot	240	475	9